ROSIE MAKINNEY

FIGHT FOR LOVE

How to Take Your Marriage Back from Porn

B&H
PUBLISHING
NASHVILLE, TENNESSEE

978-1-5359-6732-7

Published by B&H Publishing Group
Nashville, Tennessee

Dewey Decimal Classification: 176
Subject Heading: PORNOGRAPHY / MARRIAGE / HUSBANDS

Unless otherwise noted, all Scripture quotations are taken from
the Christian Standard Bible®, Copyright © 2017 by Holman Bible
Publishers. Used by permission. Christian Standard Bible® and CSB®
are federally registered trademarks of Holman Bible Publishers.

Also used: New American Standard Bible (NASB),
copyright © 1960, 1962, 1963, 1968, 1971, 1972, 1973,
1975, 1977, 1995 by The Lockman Foundation.

Also used: New International Version (NIV), NIV®
copyright ©1973, 1978, 1984, 2011 by Biblica, Inc.®
Used by permission. All rights reserved worldwide.

Also used: New King James Version (NKJV), copyright © 1982 by
Thomas Nelson. Used by permission. All rights reserved.

Also used: New English Translation (NET), copyright © 1996-2017 by
Biblical Studies Press, L.L.C. http://netbible.com All rights reserved.

Also used: New Living Translation (NLT), copyright © 1996, 2004, 2015
by Tyndale House Foundation. Used by permission of Tyndale House
Publishers, Inc., Carol Stream, Illinois 60188. All rights reserved.

Also used: King James Version (KJV), public domain.

Cover design and illustration by Micah Smith.
Author photo by Alan Fraser.

1 2 3 4 5 6 7 • 24 23 22 21 20

To all my sisters fighting in the trenches,
you are not alone.

Acknowledgments

Despite my British stiff upper lip, every time I sit down to write this section, I get emotional. The level of support I have received during the process of writing this book takes my breath away. So many writers, friends, acquaintances, and even strangers have generously poured stories, expertise, and encouragement into me. And, somehow, the comments and prayers always came at just the right time. To the many people who went out of their way to tell me they were glad I was writing this book, please know that it was your words that kept me writing mine.

To my amazing editor, Ashley Gorman, with your heart for the gospel, passion for this subject, and wisdom and expertise, I consider myself the luckiest of authors. I owe you a great debt of gratitude for how you have shaped this book, and I thank you for always going the extra mile to get things just right.

To my agent, Steve Laube, I thank you for how skillfully you guided me, and how valiantly you fought for this project. You gave me wings and the courage to use them.

To my publisher, B&H, and my incredible team—Mary Wiley, Jenaye White, Chaselynn Bowser, and Jade Novak—I am amazed by your skill, humbled by your belief in me, and grateful for your passion to get this message into the hands of women who need to hear it.

Many thanks also to Mount Hermon Christian Writers Conference for years of faithfully providing writers with inspiration, friends for life, and fertile ground for divine connections.

To the bold and brave wives, husbands, mothers, and daughters whose stories I have included in these pages, thank you for trusting me and for sharing so openly. This is your book as much as it is mine.

And now to my dear writing sisters, Ann Neumann, Holly Varni, and Wendi Lee. You guys are everything. You shaped my words, sharpened my sword, dried my tears, and made me believe I could do it. And I am sorry I made you read more about porn than anyone really needs to know.

Writing a book like this, covering so many different topics, is only possible because of the incredible work that has already been done by other fighters. I want to gratefully acknowledge fellow warrior Gary Wilson from yourbrainonporn.com, who despite persecution, tirelessly strives to promote scientific truth over lies. Also, a big thank you to his wife, Marnia Robinson, for giving me the benefit of her scientific expertise and sharp editorial eye. Here I must also mention the life-changing ministries and organizations of Josh McDowell Ministries, Beggar's Daughter, Dirty Girls Ministries, Fight the New Drug, Protect Young

Minds, and The National Coalition Against Sexual Exploitation. Keep up the good fight. We need you.

Now to my family, my deepest thanks for bearing with a highly distracted wife and mommy, a messy house, and some very interesting meals. To my two beloved boys, your endless capacity to love and be joyful is my inspiration. You are my greatest blessing and the reason I fight for a better world. To my husband, Mark, dare I say it? Without you, none of this would have been possible! Seriously, my love, thank you for making my happily-ever-after come true and for being the bravest person I know. I see you toiling relentlessly in the trenches, day after day, pushing people up into the light, and often getting kicked in the face in the process. You may not have a white horse, but you are my hero.

And finally, to the One who puts breath in my lungs, peace in my heart, and a joyful song on my lips: thank You for relentlessly pursuing me, until I came home to You.

Contents

Foreword xiii

Introduction. 1

Chapter 1: The Problem with Porn 7

Chapter 2: How Porn Hijacks the Brain 19

Chapter 3: The Faithful Response 33

Chapter 4: The Truth about Recovery 49

Chapter 5: The Tools of Recovery 63

Chapter 6: Freedom through Fellowship 93

Chapter 7: Your Healing Journey. 109

Chapter 8: Bringing Light to the Church's Fight. 125

Chapter 9: Women Who Struggle with Porn. 145

Chapter 10: Porn-Proofing Your Kids 161

Notes. 187

Foreword

For the past fifty-five years, I have led Josh McDowell Ministries to help thousands of people across the globe discover a purpose-driven, faith-based life, which includes healthy relationships and sexuality. After commissioning the most comprehensive survey of porn use within the church (The Porn Phenomenon 2016), I can say with absolute certainty that the biggest threat facing Christian marriages and families is Internet pornography. That's why I am so grateful that Rosie Makinney is empowering women to speak up and have a voice on this topic, spurring them on to take action in a healthy way. For too long, the most neglected people in the church have been the wives of porn addicts.

If we really want to change the trajectory of where porn is taking the church, we have to acknowledge that porn is not exclusively every man's battle. Porn is everyone's battle. Wives are not only deeply affected; they are vital to winning the war. They are indispensable. Instead of denying porn's presence in the home, or worse, accommodating it, what we need is an army of proactive and faith-filled spouses standing firm against the sin that enslaves their husbands' hearts and minds.

Rosie Makinney has done an excellent job in writing the recruitment manual for such an army, helping wives recognize and understand the crucial role they have to play in keeping their household porn-free.

Using neuroscience and Scripture, and unflinching honesty, Rosie brings hard facts and hard truths for these hard times. This book has a challenging message, but it is beautifully wrapped in hope and grace and gentle humor. I'd consider it essential reading for Christian wives trying to navigate life and relationships in a pornified culture. It's time to equip and encourage women to pick up their swords and join in the fight.

—Josh D. McDowell, author

Introduction

Discovering my husband was a porn addict was devastating and confusing. How could the smart, funny, kind man I had just married be hopelessly addicted to porn? Up to this point, my knowledge of sex or porn addiction was limited to tabloid scandals involving celebrities. Hardly comforting reading. Isolated in my shame, I desperately needed answers to my questions. Why did he continue to look at porn, even though he knew I hated it? Was this the reason he'd started acting differently toward me? Could it be my fault? Should I still have sex with him? Should I try to compete with what he was watching? Would I ever trust him again? Could he ever be free of porn? Was there any hope?

When my world was spinning, and my head and heart were conflicted, this is the book I needed to read. Just so you know, it's part memoir (validating the experience of living in crazy-land with an active addict), part informational (looking at the science behind porn addiction and explaining why things seem to be getting worse), and part biblical battle plan (showing how to fight lovingly and effectively for a porn-free marriage).

I wrote this book for women who are tired of feeling rejected, inadequate, and used because of their husband's porn use. Women who need to hear that their longing for emotional connection, their desire to feel cherished and adored, their hope for a truly monogamous marriage, and their need to feel valued and heard are not naïve or unrealistic. Women who refuse to accept that this is all Jesus has for them.

Do you remember—before you were hurt and rejected—how your heart's deepest desire was to be fully emotionally, spiritually, and sexually intimate with your husband? That craving was God-given. Marriage is one of the most sacred and intimate relationships we can experience here on Earth. There's a reason that Jesus calls the Church His bride.

Your desire for deep intimacy is holy and good.

You were made in the image of God, and He is all about relationships. God the Trinity is three persons in one. You can't get more intimate or relational than that! The anxiety you feel at being disconnected from your husband is a bittersweet reminder of how you were made to love and be loved. In that way, your discontentment in the way things are is actually a holy unrest, an impulse from God Himself.

You were created to be fully known, understood, and accepted.

It's tempting to think that if you could just find a way to get over yourself and be okay with your husband's porn, you would be able to feel close to him again. But the problem with this belief is that it depends on *you* and your ability to be okay with porn— and that is never going to happen. The Holy Spirit dwells within you. In the eyes of God, you and your husband are one, and by allowing porn into his mind, he is poisoning you also. Your spirit will always be distressed by the presence of evil. And evil is not something to get over in your marriage. It's something to get *out* of your marriage. The Holy Spirit isn't going to leave you alone until you address this, because He's the one who designed marriage and sexuality in the first place.

If it sounds a bit dramatic to you to call porn satanic, then brace yourself. It's time to learn the truth about what your husband is actually watching. I want you to feel righteously indignant every time you hear porn casually referred to as "the sin that all men struggle with" or mentioned in the same breath as watching too much football. Porn is literally ripping hundreds of thousands of families apart. A survey undertaken by the American Academy of Matrimonial Lawyers revealed that over half of divorce cases (56%) involved one person having an obsession with pornographic websites.[1] Yes. *Half* of divorces. How many families are being destroyed by *Monday Night Football*? Okay, maybe that's not the best example, but you get what I mean. Porn must not be swept under the rug or dismissed as "men being men." It is a lie to say that it is inherently male to arouse yourself by lusting after other women. If this were the case, it would be inherent for Jesus Himself to purposefully lust, and of course, He doesn't do that. In fact, He forbids it for any of His disciples.

Though it's certainly not all on you to "fix" your husband, you are one flesh with him, which means you *do* have a vital role to play in helping your husband become the man he was created to be, but exactly what that looks like may surprise you. In this battle against porn, knowledge is everything.

Our journey together begins with taking a good hard look at the enemy we face. You will learn why you need to take up arms, what weapons you have at your disposal, and most importantly, who you have fighting with you as your champion, because "the one who is in you is greater than the one who is in the world" (1 John 4:4).

Over the past ten years, my husband and I have had the privilege of walking alongside hundreds of couples coming out of porn addiction and into wholeness and happiness beyond their greatest expectations. This book is inspired by them and written by them, through me to you. Everyone who contributed their stories to this book did so enthusiastically and joyfully. Now that they are on the other side of recovery, all they want to do is reach out to you, give you a massive hug, and reassure you that there is hope.

So much hope.

They, like me, are living proof that you have *a living hope* in Jesus. Everyday miracles happen. I wish I could guarantee that your miracle will come in the form you want. But if you are in an abusive relationship with an unrepentant man who refuses to get help, your miracle may come in the form of strength to remove yourself and your children from further harm.

However, let me say this loud and clear: I can guarantee that educating yourself on what porn is doing to you, your marriage, and your family is not going to make things worse. It might *feel* worse, because now you are aware that porn is like a venomous snake slithering around your house, but the danger was always there. You just didn't realize it.

This book is a wake-up call to bring in the snake catcher, and block up the holes. If you want intimacy and trust back in your marriage, you (and your husband) are going to have to fight for it.

So, without further ado, let's begin by finding out why doing nothing, and hoping the issue will go away on its own, is a risky option.

CHAPTER 1

The Problem with Porn

E nough.

Not a word a bride usually says to her husband on their honeymoon. But I did.

I said it on Day Eight, one week after we'd taken our wedding vows. You see, there weren't just the two of us in the bedroom. There were three. And the third was porn. I would have called it earlier, but I was stuck on a remote Italian island (coincidently, the same one that Napoleon was exiled to as punishment).

Now I'd like to say that this remarkably assertive move was down to a strong sense of self-worth, but it wasn't. Far from it. The sad truth was, prior to becoming a Christian, I had already been in a significant long-term relationship with an unrepentant porn addict and I knew exactly how this played out. I was not going down this road again. No way. If I had to compete with porn, I knew I would lose, every time, hands down. I was already well acquainted with the all-consuming mistress of porn, and it was obvious to me that she had her hooks deep in my brand-new husband. I knew the signs. He was edgy, critical, and highly resentful. Sex was a minefield. Nothing satisfied him.

I had already learned the truth about porn the hard way. I had wasted years trying to placate, plead, and pretend porn away. This time, I was not making the same mistakes. Fortunately, this time things were different. My husband had already lost a previous marriage to porn addiction, and he was done trying to win the battle on his own. He was ready to get help.

As we entered recovery and I began educating myself about porn addiction, I was shocked and amazed to discover the extent to which porn affects the brain and negatively impacts relationships. I remember thinking, *How did I not know this information? Why is this not public knowledge? How can all these studies exist and yet the media and popular culture would have us believe that porn is harmless and good for relationships?* When I finally understood that the cause of our difficulties was neither because I was fatally flawed, nor because my husband had a serious mental health issue, I felt tremendous relief, and, for the first time, hope.

I was not crazy. He was not crazy. The problem was porn.

————

Wives have a vital role to play in the battle against porn, but in a far more proactive manner than the one the church currently promotes. Though not every church offers bad advice, unfortunately, there are many that do. And let me tell you, being non-critical, non-confrontational, and always sexually available will do nothing in terms of helping your husband break free from porn. The answer is not simply "have more sex with him" or "show up for his fantasies." In fact, this approach will actually make the problem worse, by enabling your husband's behavior to continue without him experiencing any natural consequences. Advice like this sets couples up for years, if not decades, of mistrust and hostility.

The truth that many churches seem unaware of—with much "men only" teachings on porn—is that married men do not often seek recovery unprompted. Though husbands *should* seek out repentance and change on their own, the unfortunate truth—one my husband and I have concluded, after dedicating our ministry to this over many years and helping hundreds of couples—is this: the catalyst that propels the vast majority of husbands into recovery is their wife forcing the issue. However, it usually takes many long years of suffering for a wife to finally reach that point. And the longer a wife endures, the more traumatized she becomes, and the harder her journey back to a place of health, trust, and reconciliation will be.

According to Josh McDowell, prominent apologist and author, "Pornography's the greatest threat to the cause of Christ in the history of the world."[1] Fifty-five percent of married Christian men look at porn at least monthly, and one in ten looks at porn at least daily.[2] Yet only 7 percent of churches have a ministry program for those struggling with porn.[3] This leaves millions of Christian men struggling on their own, and millions of heartbroken wives wondering how best to love their husbands: *Should I get angry? Should I hold my tongue? Should I try to spice things up? Or should I simply just get over myself and stop making such a fuss? Should I deny it's happening or accommodate it?*

Without informed, biblical advice, wives are often left in a spiral of self-sabotaging, self-defeating efforts to fix their relationship.

> *My pastor's wife informed me that my role as helpmate was to support my husband without judgment or criticism. Gentleness, grace, and sexual availability would solve all our problems. If I loved him enough, he would stop using porn. So, for the next few months, I made no demands on him and was always positive. It was not always easy to ignore his coldness and continue to be sexual with him, but I was determined. My efforts were rewarded with an Internet history that revealed he was using porn whenever I left the house.*
>
> *I confronted him, we argued, he promised to stop, we tried again.*
>
> *And again.*
>
> *And again.*
>
> *We started seeing a Christian marriage therapist, and she helped me understand how men struggle with porn, and that my anger and bitterness was not helpful. I worked hard on my forgiveness and holding my tongue. Then one night I woke up*

and found him on his phone. The look on his face told me everything I needed to know. Even after everything we had been through, he still chose porn over me. He would always choose porn over me. (Anna, age 32)

With the information she had, Anna tried everything she knew to get porn out of her marriage. She tried so hard, and for so long, but, no matter what approach she took to get her husband to stop, nothing made any difference. However, as traumatic and painful as Anna's experience was, it did get her to a point of saying "Enough," and this was the turning point in their marriage. Anna gave her husband an ultimatum—he could have porn or her, but not both. Fortunately, her husband chose recovery, and they finally received the help and support they needed. Their story has a happy ending, or rather a happy new beginning. Yet, the years Anna spent enabling her husband's addiction took their toll on her heart and her trust. Their journey back to a place of restoration was long and difficult.

At some point in the future, public awareness about the harmful effects of porn will become widespread, just as it did with smoking. But, until that time, it is down to us to educate ourselves, and each other.

The Facts about Porn

Porn Creates Dissatisfaction in and out of the Bedroom

If you feel sexually inadequate and body-conscious when you are being sexual with your husband, be reassured that your instincts are working fine. It has been proven that the more porn a man watches, the more likely he is to be thinking about porn to maintain his arousal when having sex.[4] You are not being paranoid. Subconsciously, or consciously, your husband is negatively comparing you. In one study it was found that both men and women felt less satisfied with their partner's looks, affection, and sexual performance after being exposed to nonviolent porn for only one hour a week for six weeks.[5] And compared with the amount of porn most users consume, that is not a lot of porn. A brain imprinted with unlimited fantasy women—who are always full of desire and who never place any emotional demands—is not capable of being satisfied with just one real woman.

And if that wasn't bad enough, the damage is not limited to what's going on inside the mind. The body is also affected in major ways. The dreadful irony of watching porn is that while it creates higher sexual desire, it also makes it harder to become aroused and/or sexually satisfied with a real person. Just like cigarettes, porn really does need to come with a public health warning. A Cambridge University study found that sixty percent of men with compulsive sexual behavior experienced low sex drive or erectile function.[6] Another study revealed that of those who viewed seven or more hours of pornography per week, 71 percent reported sexual dysfunctions, and 33 percent reported delayed ejaculation.[7]

This is the reason many husbands don't touch their wives for months. Or why others find it so difficult to become aroused, or have trouble being satisfied. In the absence of a public health campaign, I need you to hear this loud and clear.

It's not you; it's porn.

The toxicity of porn also extends far beyond the bedroom. Married couples who use pornography more often report lower satisfaction with their decision-making as a couple.[8] Pornography use is strongly and negatively related to marital quality over time. The longer porn is present in a marriage, the unhappier you both become.[9] And it doesn't take long for things to escalate quickly. When a husband or a wife starts watching porn, they double their chance of getting divorced within the following two years. The risk of divorce is even greater for younger married couples.[10] Engaging in pornographic use also makes it three times more likely for a man to have an affair.[11]

Porn Destroys Authenticity and Intimacy

Even when it is unspoken, pornography creates a wedge between husband and wife. Not only is it hard to be authentic and present when hiding such a big secret, but after the pleasure-numbing high of porn, everything else in life can seem unsatisfying, stressful, and irritating. Everyday challenges and frustrations become easily overblown. Do you feel like your husband is constantly unhappy with you, even snapping at you for minor inconveniences? Do you feel like you can never measure up? Do you feel that even when he is with you he doesn't want to be there?

You are not alone.

Many wives report feeling like they are walking on eggshells. As soon as they bring something up, it is twisted around and the blame is put back on them. Psychologists know this tactic as "gas-lighting." In this situation, a wife learns that speaking what's on her heart normally comes back to bite her. So, she grits her teeth and hides her hurt. She doesn't share how deeply dishonored she feels, or how confused she is about why he keeps looking at porn even though he knows it hurts her.

Now there are two people hiding in the marriage, seeking outward (and false) harmony over truth. Both feel like actors in their own lives, inauthentic and distant from everybody. This is no long-term solution. The answer is not to find a way to manage these painful emotions. Pain motivates us to make changes. When we hide our hurt and anger—and continue to be sexual with our husbands as if nothing is wrong—we reinforce the lie that porn is acceptable and benign. By holding back our righteous indignation, we prevent God from using our voice to speak truth and life to our husbands.

Porn Is Idolatry

Just because today's carved idol fits in a back pocket and is worshipped in secret does not make it any less sinful in the sight of God. The consequences of idolatry are no less serious. Sexual immorality robs us of our inheritance of power, peace, and authority here on earth.

> For know and recognize this: Every sexually
> immoral or impure or greedy person, who is
> an idolater, does not have an inheritance in the
> kingdom of Christ and of God. (Eph. 5:5)

It's time for Christian women to stand up and say "Enough."
Enough blaming ourselves, enough trying to compete, enough
burying our heads in the sand, enough hiding our hearts, enough
keeping our voices silent on the matter, and enough waiting for
him to change. If your marriage has been hijacked by porn,
the most faithful way to love your husband is to send a strong
message of zero tolerance. And remember, it's not you versus him.
It's not *your* will be done. It's *God's*. By drawing a line in the
sand, you are helping your husband follow what *God* says—not
what you say, not what culture says, and not what porn says.
God has an opinion on our sexuality. More than that, God has a
design for it and a will for it, and it's right to fight to stay within
the lines of it:

> For this is God's will, your sanctification: that
> you keep away from sexual immorality, that
> each of you knows how to control his own body
> in holiness and honor, not with lustful pas-
> sions, like the Gentiles, who don't know God.
> (1 Thess. 4:3–5)

Confronting the issue of porn in your marriage requires
faith, especially in the early stages when things don't seem "that
bad." The world, your husband, and possibly your church, may
not initially agree with you making waves. But God doesn't ask

His children to do easy things; He asks us to do the hard things. God is glorified when we show the world that we trust Him enough to work in us and through us.

In Judges 6:25, God asked Gideon to tear down his father's altar to Baal and the Asherah pole they worshipped. Gideon obeyed the Lord, but, because he was afraid of his family and the townspeople, he did it at night rather than the daytime. Gideon was visited by an angel—he knew he was working for God—but he was *still* afraid. Can you relate with that at all? I know I can. See, God doesn't need you to be perfectly fearless before He'll use your obedience. He works through us just as we are. He honors our obedience, even if we are shaky as we obey. And here's the best bit. After he was done, Gideon used the wood of the Asherah pole to build a fire upon which to burn his sacrifice. Gideon took what was once used to worship Satan and used it to glorify God. Isn't that beautiful?

Time and time again, ordinary people in the Bible were used by God in audacious ways to accomplish His will. The same God is at work in us today.

> For God has not given us a spirit of fear, but one
> of power, love, and sound judgment. (2 Tim. 1:7)

Do you sense how God is working behind the scenes in your own story? Can you see Him pointing out an idol in your home that He wants torn down? Do you feel like God is using this time to call you back to Him, to strengthen and prepare you for a time such as this?

"For the LORD has called you, like a wife deserted
and wounded in spirit, a wife of one's youth when
she is rejected," says your God. (Isa. 54:6)

Evil has infiltrated our households and is infecting our husbands and children, and perhaps even ourselves (see chapter 9 for
that). Is God really asking us to be silent? To sit back and watch
our marriages and lives disintegrate? Or is He calling us to rise
up and tear down the idols of porn within our homes?

We cannot afford to sit around and wait for help that may or
may not arrive; we have to pick up our sledgehammers now. As
we shall learn in the next chapter, when it comes to the impact
of porn on the brain, time is of the essence.

CHAPTER 2

♥ ♥ ♥

How Porn
Hijacks the Brain

Y ou want me to spend New Year's Eve where?"
    After our disastrous honeymoon, I thought nothing
my husband could do would shock me. I was wrong. After four
months of being cooped up in a tiny vacation rental with him
going through withdrawal, I was not in the mood for any more of
his surprises. Did I mention that I had quit a job I adored and left
my entire support network six thousand miles behind in the UK
in order to get married? That Christmas I teetered on the edge of
a very dark place. So, let's just say I was expecting a nice dinner,
at the very least, come New Year's Eve. What I got instead was
an all-expenses paid retreat in the beautiful redwoods of Santa
Cruz just him, me, and sixty members of Sex and Love Addicts
Anonymous.

    Perfect.

Could life get any better?

When we arrived at the retreat center and took our luggage out of the car, Mark accidentally slammed the trunk on my head. This was the straw that broke my back, as it were, and I collapsed into a muddy puddle in tears. It felt like he would never stop hurting me. How did I get here? I used to go to glamorous parties at New Year. Now I was reduced to attending conventions of sweaty perverts in metaphorical trench coats.

To my utter astonishment, that weekend was the most pivotal in my life. Never had I been in the presence of such raw, honest, and openly broken people. They were funny and sweet and their stories were achingly sad. We shared and cried and laughed so hard that we cried again. I heard the pain of the addicts and began to see my husband as not just a sinner but also a victim too. For the first time I tasted the sweetness of authentic fellowship and I was hooked. I never knew that people actually talked about real stuff outside of movies. And what of New Year's Eve itself? It was utterly hysterical. I loved every crazy minute. If you have never been to a talent show by a bunch of sex addicts, you haven't lived.

Directly or indirectly, every beautiful brave soul I met that weekend had had their lives devastated by sex and/or porn addiction. When I returned home, it struck me just how blatantly and casually porn use is encouraged in popular culture, even being used as a marketing ploy. Breathtaking landscapes are considered "earth porn," inspirational quotes are dubbed "word porn," and passionate foodies are encouraged to click, drool, and repeat at certain "food porn" websites. However, while the content of these aspirational websites, or Pinterest boards, or Instagram images is harmless, normalizing and idealizing the word *porn*—and the habits associated with it—is most definitely not. Porn is not a harmless, idealized version of sex. It is an artificial, supernormal stimulus that hijacks and rewires the brain.

What's a Supernormal Stimulus?

In the 1950s Nikolaas Tinbergen, a Nobel Prize–winning biologist, made a striking discovery. He found that he could create "artificial" stimuli that were stronger than animals' original instincts.[1] Birds would prefer to sit on constructed plaster eggs if they were larger, had more defined markings, or were more saturated in color. For example, the bird's own pale, dappled eggs would be rejected in favor of neon ones with black spots. Territorial male stickleback fish would ignore real males and attack wooden models of male fish with redder undersides. And male butterflies would try to mate with cardboard dummy butterflies with more defined markings in preference to real females.

Why am I talking about birds and butterflies? Well, Tinbergen was able to alter the behavior of these animals with a new "super" stimulus that tripped their instinctual response more powerfully than the real thing. Because they couldn't say no to the fake stimulus, the animals' new behavior threatened their very survival. Becoming so enamored with the artificial and enhanced features of their lifeless "mates," real mating, with real birds and fish and butterflies, was now jeopardized.

Advancing technology has created a similar situation for us. The reward center of our brains has been hijacked by the supernormal stimulus of Internet porn to the point where it can become preferable to sex—or any sort of intimacy—with a real partner.

Porn hijacks the reward center of the brain.

On a high shelf in my pantry I have a glass jar full of shiny tokens that I use to reward my kids. Whether it's music practice without resistance, or chores without tears, or simply refraining from teasing each other for a whole afternoon, I use tokens to reinforce behavior that I want repeated. When the kids have collected enough, they can trade them for something pleasurable; maybe a trip to the ice-cream parlor or a favorite TV show.

Our brains work in a similar way. Deep in our brain is a primitive reward circuitry that produces dopamine and a cocktail of other "feel good" chemicals every time we do something that theoretically furthers our survival.[2] When we do an activity like eating or having sex, we are biologically rewarded. This motivates us to repeat the behavior. The trouble is, much like my parenting, the system isn't foolproof—it doesn't always reward the right things. It can be hijacked by counterfeit substitutes. You don't need me to tell you that high-calorie foods produce more of the "feel good" neurotransmitter dopamine. Just thinking about donuts makes you happy, right? But, although a diet consisting of donuts and burgers might feel good for a while, you know long term it's going to lead to a whole host of health issues.

The case is similar with porn. Except with porn there is one crucial difference—one that makes it dangerous from the very first bite. Porn is not simply sexual junk food; it is poison.

As you watch porn, your brain is tricked into pumping out the same "feel good" cocktail as it would when seeing or physically engaging with a real mate.[3] However, if you were having a real romantic encounter, eventually you would feel satisfied. There is a natural built in "off switch" for natural pleasures like food and sex: dopamine stops being produced.[4]

Yet, with Internet porn there is no "off switch."[5] The dopamine just keeps on coming. You literally can binge for days. All you need to do to keep dopamine endlessly surging is click on something new, something more stimulating.[6] The key here is novelty or surprise. In one session of porn you can click on hundreds of "potential mating partners" and flood your brain with dopamine. How can any one woman compete with that experience?

Too much of a good thing: Porn eventually numbs the reward circuit.

How does the brain respond to excessive, unnatural, sustained pulses of dopamine? Just like my kids cover their ears when a fire truck screams past us, the brain responds in a similar way by effectively "covering" its dopamine receptors and gradually numbing its pleasure response.[7] Porn that once provided an intense thrill may not even register now. Users often find they need more and more stimulation to experience the same high. They are compelled to either increase the amount of time spent viewing or to seek out things that are novel or surprising as a way to jack up their lagging dopamine.[8]

The point to remember is that porn use often escalates to darker, more extreme material. When what is being watched no longer satisfies as it once did, users need to find something that pushes the envelope a little bit more, and a little bit more, and a little bit more. Usually, people don't start using porn to watch overwhelmingly vulgar or violent material. They start with what society would deem "normal" types, and then they slowly escalate to worse and worse material, as they need to keep up the dopamine rush. As a wife, what you need to know is this: the longer you stay silent, the deeper into his pit your husband will descend.

> *Watching two people have sex soon became boring; I needed to up the ante. I hunted for something different, something taboo. The problem was that whatever new thing I'd find, it never satisfied for long and back on the hunt I'd go. With the Internet there was always another, even more shocking, avenue to explore. For me, it was less about the content and more about the hunt to find "it"—the bit of film that would really do it for me. A frenzy would descend on me and I would just blow past any sense of right or wrong.* (Jackson, age 30)

In addition to switching off (or numbing) pleasure receptors, the brain also has another trick up its sleeve to deal with runaway levels of dopamine. When a critical level of stimulation is reached, the brain releases a chemical called "cyclic adenosine monophosphate response element binding protein," also known as CREB.[9] CREB functions like a set of brakes, inhibiting the reward circuit and helping people come back down to earth after a pleasurable experience.[10] Without it, we would never make it out of the dining room or bedroom and be able to get on with our lives. A very helpful chemical—until it comes to porn.

Repeated porn use can create a build-up of CREB, causing a baseline change in a person's reward circuit.[11] It dulls enjoyment of not just porn, but anything and everything. Nothing gives the same pleasure it once did. The laughter of children no longer steals the heart. Physical intimacy with a spouse feels duller and less pleasurable. The satisfaction of a job well done at work no longer feels rewarding. Passion for hobbies and interests fade. The whole world, and every experience in it, feels lackluster. This state is called "tolerance," and is often present in addictions, creating a craving for more intense stimulation. It is the reason why addicts appear bored, detached, and depressed with real life.[12] They are unable to feel normal. Only their preferred "drug" promises relief.

> The high of Internet porn was so intense that everything else dulled in comparison— things that I used to enjoy were ridiculously mundane in comparison to porn. My job, my wife, my kids, hobbies, life itself had become

unutterably boring. Nothing matched up to
the intensity of porn. (Brian, age 48)

God, in His wisdom and goodness, knew what He was
doing when He wired our brains the way He did, with checks
and balances in perfect order, to enable us to enjoy food, sex,
relationships, work, and play in a way that brings true and lasting pleasure. Going outside of God's design and engaging with
porn and other drugs compromises any chance at true happiness.

Porn addiction is a real, debilitating disease, not a fabricated
condition created by money-hungry, sex-addiction therapists.
Neither does the term provide an excuse for a lack of willpower.
Along with gaming addiction and gambling addiction, porn
addiction is an example of a process addiction where the "drug"
is produced by the brain itself instead of being injected, ingested,
or smoked.[13]

If you remember only one thing from this chapter, remember
this: Internet pornography is highly and dangerously addictive.

Gimme, gimme, gimme: Porn creates addictive pathways in the brain.

Whenever I buy chocolate Popsicles, it's like a magic spell
has been cast over my six-year-old. From the moment they are
placed in the shopping cart, he becomes all-consumed with the
thought of them. Nothing else matters. Everything else pales in
comparison. The association between Popsicles and pleasure is so
strongly ingrained in his brain that if I were to give him a choice
between his beloved toy cat and a Popsicle, poor Flopsy would be
traded in a heartbeat.

He has already learned life lesson number one: chocolate makes everything better.

Humans thrive and survive by building and strengthening learning pathways in the brain. It is how God designed us to hone our skills and make everyday tasks more efficient.[14] Whether it's hunting dinner on the plain, playing the piano, or practicing a sport, our brains process information and control our bodies much faster using these neural pathways. The more often we practice, the more automatic our actions become.

When I learned to drive a stick shift, I remember being overwhelmed by each hand and foot doing a different job simultaneously. My instructor would regularly stop the car and hand out candy when it all got too much for me (and probably him too). Now, thanks to my long-suffering instructor and a pushy little protein called "DeltaFosB," driving is automatic. I mention DeltaFosB not to impress you with my fancy knowledge of neurochemicals, but because it plays a very important role in the hijacking of a brain on porn.

DeltaFosB's job is to strengthen neural pathways,[15] and, as addictions develop, it goes into supercharge mode.[16] During porn consumption, extra amounts of DeltaFosB are produced, which create the equivalent of an asphalt paver in your brain. The neural pathway connecting the promised reward to porn is made so durable that other pleasures may have difficulty competing with it.

I was on day 9 of porn sobriety. I had a good night's sleep. I'd been for a jog. I was feeling good, better than I had done for months.

It made no sense to me why feeling happy should make me crave porn so badly, but it did. Feeling good, bad, happy, sad or mad, it didn't seem to matter. All of it led me right back to porn. (Josh, age 25)

This is especially true during adolescence when the teenage brain releases higher levels of dopamine and produces even more DeltaFosB.[17] DeltaFosB is chillingly referred to as "a molecular switch for addiction,"[18] because a big enough build-up can switch on genes that create long-term cravings, driving the user back for more.

Anything can become a trigger for porn cravings.

DeltaFosB is a conscientious worker. When you do something that feels really rewarding, it's going to make sure that you don't forget about it anytime soon. And in addition to creating the connection between porn and pleasure, it also builds connections to everything associated with it.[19] In the same way smokers may be triggered by the smell of cigarettes, or an alcoholic by passing an old drinking den, porn users can be triggered by just being in the room where they watch it, or the night of the week when their spouse goes out, or even just thinking about a certain porn scene. Porn addiction is one of the hardest addictions to beat because porn addicts have the equivalent of an open bar in their head.

I didn't need to find a dealer, spend money, or leave my living room. All I had to do was close my eyes and my favorite drug was coursing through my head, the deeply embedded memories of all the porn I've watched could be easily recalled for an instant high. (Sonny, age 53)

Porn changes your sexual tastes.

Porn users may think they are simply being entertained but watching porn is not a neutral experience; it shapes the users' sexual tastes. All the while porn is viewed, the brain is busily building connections between feelings of arousal and whatever's happening on the screen.[20]

Let's pause for a moment and consider what this means for a heavy porn user who is compelled to seek out darker and more extreme pornographic material in order to sustain arousal. Before he knows it, he may find his sexual tastes have changed and he is aroused by material that used to disgust him; material that is inappropriate, unethical and/or illegal. All too often, porn users end up in over their heads and families are torn apart. In one study, half of the porn users surveyed reported that they had escalated to porn they once considered uninteresting or "disgusting."[21] Standing up to porn use is not about being a prude, it's about being prudent.

If porn is an issue in your marriage, you don't need me to tell you that something feels off with your sex-life. Heavy porn use typically manifests in one of two very different ways. Either a husband's sex drive goes through the roof, causing a wife to feel pressured to have sex far more frequently that she would like and/or to partake in acts commonly featured in porn. Or he consistently avoids and rejects her sexually, sometimes even turning the situation around and blaming her for his lack of interest. Either way, a wife inevitably ends up feeling like his disappointment, dissatisfaction, or disinterest is her fault.

Porn causes a decline in executive functioning.

Porn overuse does not just hijack the reward center of the brain but also the command center—the part of the brain that helps us make reasoned, thoughtful decisions.

When both my children were preschoolers and their pre-frontal cortexes were still very much developing, I had to help them set goals, assess risks, keep on task, inhibit the impulse to eat pennies, and reflect on their decision to squirt Mommy's expensive hand cream down the sink. I was acting as their sur-rogate pre-frontal cortex, filtering information and guiding them toward decisions that would be good for their survival and well-being.

When they reach the age of twenty-five, their prefrontal cortexes will be fully developed and they will have "executive control" of the processes going on in their brains. They will be able to do abstract thinking, set goals, solve problems, regulate behavior, and suppress emotions, impulses, and urges for themselves. Hopefully. That is, as long as they stay away from addiction and aren't involved in any head-on collisions.

Both heavy porn use and head trauma can cause a condition called "hypofrontality" in the pre-frontal cortex.[22] Basically, this term translates as the inhibition of many of the higher func-tions of the prefrontal cortex. With hypofrontality, a person has trouble thinking logically. They become less able to weigh consequences and situations, and override cravings. What was once considered simply a desire is now experienced as a compelling and urgent need.

In other words, the little voice in your head saying "let's just think about this for a minute, you know what happened last time," is drowned out by another voice shouting "GO FOR IT, DO IT, DO IT, IT'LL STOP THE PAIN!" Even when experience teaches that continuing to use porn is going to have serious consequences, the weakened impulse control cannot compete against the cravings.

There is no point cajoling or waiting for your husband to want to get better if his brain has been hijacked by porn. At this point, he doesn't need a pep talk, he needs the equivalent of Navy Seals to bust him out of some seriously impaired thinking. In fact, though God can certainly grant him repentance in his mind and heart, you need to remember that his decision-making ability—whether that be small decisions or the decision to watch porn today—is seriously compromised.

If your husband was regularly sneaking out of bed and snorting cocaine, I doubt you would be wasting time blaming yourself or attempting to "cure" him with more marital sex as a means to outdo the high he is on. And you certainly wouldn't be persuaded into snorting it with him. On top of this, you wouldn't treat him as if he could just "will" his way out of it or simply choose to stop the madness tomorrow with no outside support. You need to approach porn in exactly the same way. The answer is not to accommodate it, compete with it, or watch it with your husband to "spice up" your bedroom experience. Nor is it not to wait and see, hoping he'll make the kind of rational decisions he was making before he started this. Both faith and science tell us that engaging in pornography is not just taboo; it's damaging the brain, imparing the ability to relate and make good decisions.

And Now for Some Good News!

It is not too late. The brain is plastic. Damage caused by porn is not permanent; it is reversible. By draining the brain of porn, your husband will gradually regain his executive functioning,[23] his cravings will diminish, and he will lose sensitivity to pornographic cues.[24] He can regain the ability to fully feel and enjoy his life again.

By saying "enough" to porn, you are not simply fighting for your marriage; you're preventing further harm to your husband's brain and striving to reverse any impairment. You are also calling him back to the Lord. Early intervention is tough love. But to a man in captivity, it is exactly the kind of love he needs.

CHAPTER 3

♥　♥　♥

The Faithful Response

A few years ago, I visited a large church to hear a sermon on pornography. A few rows in front of me sat a married couple who were having difficulties because of the husband's compulsive porn use. During his talk the pastor exhorted wives in the congregation to be understanding of their husbands' struggles, and to help the situation by making themselves more sexually available.

As I watched the wife's head droop, tears filled my eyes. I knew exactly how their conversation on the way home was going to go, and it broke my heart. Long after the service finished, I remained in my seat, silently weeping. No matter how understanding she was, or how many times she had sex, things were only going to get worse for her—and for all the other wives in the same situation listening to this message.

Now, please, don't misunderstand me. I am not in any way saying the pastor deliberately gave unhelpful advice. Here was a great pastor, bravely and boldly tackling a tough subject. His desire was to help—he wanted to see people set free. He just didn't know how. Most of the bad advice given to wives is well-meaning. Of course, there are occasions where isolated Scripture passages are taken out of context and used to force wives to submit to certain sexual demands, or to stop them complaining about porn use, but that is not bad advice. That is spiritual abuse. What I'm talking about is the misapplication of Scripture concerning the submission of wives in situations where compulsive porn use is an issue.

In Ephesians 5 Paul tells women to submit to their husbands.

> Wives, submit to your husbands as to the Lord,
> because the husband is the head of the wife
> as Christ is the head of the church. He is the
> Savior of the body. Now as the church submits
> to Christ, so also wives are to submit to their
> husbands in everything. (vv. 22–24)

Many commentaries agree that this is not a value judgment on the wife's importance, dignity, or worth, but an establishment of family order, as per God's design. The husband has a leadership role as the spiritual head of the family. The purpose of leadership is to protect and bless those under the leader's authority, not to benefit the one in authority. Indeed, the following exhortation to husbands is perhaps even more challenging. "Husbands, love your wives, just as Christ loved the church and gave himself for her" (Eph. 5:25). In order to become servant-leaders, like Christ, husbands must be willing to literally die for their wives. The envisaged relationship between husband and wife is not one of Master and Servant, but of Lover and Beloved.

Problems occur when submission is presented to wives as simply obeying. Submission and obedience are two very different things. You can certainly obey without submitting—you only need to watch a child's forced apologies to see this—but, is it possible to submit without obeying?

The answer is yes.

Submission is a heart attitude where a wife freely shares her opinions and wisdom, and ultimately respects that her husband will take her input into account along with his own, and make the right decisions for both of them. However, in cases where a husband asks a wife to do something contrary to the Word of God, she has a duty to decline. Obedience to God takes precedence over obedience to anyone else, including a husband.

The wife's friends or church elders rarely advise her to do the wrong thing, but neither do they advise her to do the right thing. Again, bad advice is not usually a product of malicious intent; it is simply due to a lack of education. In certain instances, the appropriate advice to give is quite clear. For example, should a woman being coerced into re-enacting painful, unethical, or degrading porn ask whether to continue, the correct response is clearly "no." But what do you say to a wife whose husband keeps promising to stop but never does, or one who wonders if she is responsible for the problem? What do you say to the wife who has been sexually ignored by her husband for years? What do you advise her to do if the porn problem is still in a less-extreme phase and isn't wrecking their world just yet?

It's tricky, isn't it? With porn, there isn't a one size response fits all.

Or is there?

God's attitude toward sexual immorality is unequivocal and unwavering. "For this is God's will, your sanctification: that you keep away from sexual immorality, that each of you knows how to control his own body in holiness and honor" (1 Thess. 4:3–4). He does not make exceptions if a man is going through a tough time at work, or if there is a new baby in the house, or the wife has supposedly "let herself go." There is no differentiation made between lusting in the mind and acting it out. "But I tell you, everyone who looks at a woman lustfully has already committed adultery with her in his heart" (Matt. 5:28).

No matter how infrequent the usage, or how tame the material (for now), or how "guaranteed" it is that the porn participants themselves are over-age consenting adults, there is no way that pornographic use can be considered acceptable in the eyes of God. Among many things, looking at porn *is* looking at a person lustfully. And God hasn't changed His mind on whether or not He thinks that is okay. And it's not just the New Testament that tells us this. Time after time in the Old Testament, we are shown the swift and brutal consequences of sexual immorality.

> Let us not commit sexual immorality as some
> of them did, and in a single day twenty-three
> thousand people died. (1 Cor. 10:8)

Likewise, Sodom and Gomorrah and the surrounding towns committed sexual immorality
and perversions, and serve as an example by
undergoing the punishment of eternal fire.
(Jude 7)

It is not enough to counsel wives to avoid doing the wrong things (i.e., stop competing with porn, and stop silently condoning it). Wives must also be encouraged to do the right things in line with the will of God.

So, what, according to the Bible, are the right things to do? What should a godly wife do when the lifestyle of her husband, her earthly authority, is in direct opposition to the Word of God?

What the Bible Says

To help us answer this question, let's take a moment and look at a couple of occasions when Peter and John faced a similar choice between obeying their earthly authorities or their heavenly Father. Despite Peter's own clear instruction to "submit to every human authority because of the Lord, whether to the emperor as the supreme authority or to the governors" (1 Pet. 2:13–14a), we also see him repeatedly acting against the Jewish leadership. In Acts 4:18 when the priests, scribes, and elders ordered Peter and John not to speak or teach at all in the name of Jesus, this is how they answered them: "Whether it's right in the sight of God for us to listen to you rather than to God, you decide; for we are unable to stop speaking about what we have seen and heard" (4:19–20). And again in chapter 5, even after they had been thrown in jail, they still insisted, "We must obey God rather than people" (v. 29).

So how does a wife submit to her husband but still obey God in this situation?

Now let's dig in further in 1 Peter and see what he says in chapter 3, verse 1, which talks directly to wives about how to respond to husbands who are disobedient to the Word.

> In the same way, wives, submit yourselves to your own husbands so that, even if some disobey the word, they may be won over without a word by the way their wives live when they observe your pure, reverent lives. (1 Pet. 3:1–2)

While acknowledging that wives should submit themselves under the authority and protection of their husbands, Peter is reminding wives that their primary submission is to God, who commands them to remain *pure and reverent* in the presence of a disobedient husband. They are not to capitulate to enter into the ungodly things their husbands may be engaging in. Their lives should serve as a reminder that when it comes to being with those things or being with God, they are with God. But that's not all Peter says. Just look at what he says can be accomplished through a God-fearing wife's actions. By remaining obedient to the Lord, a wife can aid in bringing her husband to repentance. And if that isn't a wonderful message of hope, I don't know what is! You are not merely a side note in your husband's story, you have

an up-front central role to play in God's plan for his redemption
and restoration!

What does pure conduct look like?

When you think of the words *pure* or *chaste*, does an image
of a lovely young woman in a medieval gown holding a tapestry
hoop spring to mind, or is it just me? In a world where tapestry
has been replaced by Tinder, what could "pure" possibly look
like today?

The word *pure* comes from the Greek word *hagnos*. This can
also be translated as "clean, innocent, and modest." In a nutshell,
God is telling you to keep yourself clean and pure. In the context of a marriage where compulsive porn use is an issue, your
"wifely duty" is not to make your husband feel better about his
struggles, but to protect your heart, and mind, and body from
being polluted. Take whatever steps you need to keep yourself
emotionally, spiritually, and physically "clean." Ask yourself the
tough questions. Is becoming one with a man who has just filled
his mind with pornographic images keeping yourself pure? Is
watching it with him a way to keep your own mind and heart
pure? Is accommodating it in your house a God-honoring, good
idea? You decide. Pray about it and seek the Word; the Holy
Spirit will guide you.

Despite what anyone says, if you decide that keeping yourself
undefiled from porn means not having sex with your husband
when he watches it, you are not being punitive, or unloving;
this is you obeying the Word of God. Remember: the Bible does
not say that your husband will be won over by attending a Bible

study, or meeting weekly with an accountability partner; it says
he will be won over by *your pure* heart and behavior. God has
placed you in a position of unique influence with your husband
and has chosen you as His instrument of healing. Step into that.

And what about the being reverent or respectful part?

Interestingly, the Greek word *phobos* in 1 Peter 3:2 has been
translated in three different ways. Each has a slightly difference
inference.

> ". . . as they observe your chaste and *respectful*
> behavior." (NASB)

> ". . . when they observe your pure, *reverent*
> lives." (CSB)

> ". . . when they observe your chaste conduct
> *accompanied by fear*." (NKJV)

Many commentaries state that "respectful behavior" found
in many translations refers to a "respect of one's husband."
This certainly got me thinking. How is a wife supposed to set
boundaries in order to keep herself "pure" while still remaining
respectful to her husband's wishes? I know wives who have
wrestled with this tension for years, and it is this, more than
anything else, for which they sought guidance.

The more I meditated on this verse, the more I became
convinced that there had to be something I was missing. In
my experience, the Word of God comforts and clarifies, not

confuses. So, after a few days of head scratching, I decided to reach out for help.

It's all Greek to me.

I approached Dr. Galen K. Johnson, professor at Liberty University, to help me dig about in the original Greek text of 1 Peter 3. Without revealing the reason for my inquiry, I asked him what he thought about the translation of the word *phobos* in this verse. What he came back with blew my mind. This is what he said.

First, *phobos* in this context does not mean respect, it means fear. Or to be more precise, the experience of being put in great reverential fear or terror. Secondly, the fear does not belong to the wife. It actually belongs to the husband.

Did you have to read that twice? I did.

When I pressed Dr. Johnson to prove his claims, he patiently explained that Greek is an inflected language, which means that translation is not based upon the sequential ordering of words but the declensions of nouns that determine the translation of the whole sentence. Greek, just like every other language, apart from English, has what is called "grammatical gender." Words are assigned male or female pronouns, or word affixes, which are completely unrelated to biology. Basically, the way we can tell which parts of a Greek sentence go together is by looking at the grammatical gender of the words. Words of the same gender go together, and they don't have to be adjacent.

Look at this literal English rendering of the Greek of 1 Peter 3:2. The bold words are grammatically masculine, and the underlined words are grammatically feminine.

> when they **observing** <u>of-the</u> in fear <u>pure</u>
> <u>behavior</u> of-you

Here we can see that **in fear** modifies the verb **observing**, which has the husband as the subject. It is clearly not the wives who are supposed to be in fear; it is unrepentant husbands. This shift in emphasis is monumental. *<u>The key to a husband's trans-</u>* *<u>formation is his experience of fear when he observes his wife's higher</u>* *<u>standards of moral purity</u>*.

Here is the NKJV translation rewritten to more accurately reflect the correct application of "in fear."

> Wives, likewise, be submissive to your own
> husbands, that even if some do not obey the
> word, they, without a word, may be won by the
> conduct of their wives, when they in fear wit-
> ness your chaste conduct.

Doesn't this make you want to jump up, fist pumping, but also drop to your knees? Here we see a crystal clear, straightforward instruction to wives to pursue "chaste conduct," and leave God to do the rest. Praise Jesus! There is no tension between submitting to God and submitting to your husband when his wishes line up with God.

Note, all is accomplished "without a word." No need to explain yourself. You are simply obeying the Word of God. Oh, praise the Lord for no more exhausting emotional scenes. No more persuading, or pleading or begging him to stop. God is telling you to save your breath. It is not your words that will have impact; it is your actions. If you have fallen into a pattern of placating, soothing, or arguing because of porn, you may be surprised how quickly disengaging from the craziness will yield results.

By relinquishing your attempts to control your husband and focusing instead on obeying God, you will not only relieve yourself of a massive burden, but you'll also set your compass to actual recovery. But keeping yourself pure from porn requires more from you than simply staying away from porn and not accommodating it in your own mind. You are required to actively engage in the battle. You are commanded to rise up and tear down the idol in your household. This is what wielding an axe looks like:

1. State that you will no longer ignore or tolerate porn use in your marriage.
2. State that you would like both of you to seek help from someone who has experience of dealing with porn addiction, and if he is unwilling, you will be seeking help alone.
3. Find and join a support group for wives of porn/sex addicts in your area, or online.
4. Fix your eyes upon the Lord, and clothe yourself in the armor of God. (As a side note, I wish Priscilla Shirer's study guide

Armor of God had been available when I was
going through this. It's so powerful.)

If the thought of confronting your husband and being so
forthright is daunting, here's the good news: no one is more
qualified for this job than you. As per God's design and plan,
you have a unique position of influence with your husband.
Although it might not look, or indeed feel, like it at the moment,
the husband God chose for you needs you to stand firm on this
issue. So, step up and be the bravest, most loving, most faithful
helpmate you can be.

I wish I could give you a step-by-step guide on how to convince your husband that his life, your life, and the lives of your
kids will be much better off if he gets the help he needs, but I
can't. There is no recipe. However, what I can do is remind you
that now you are obeying God, His hand is firmly guiding you,
and you are not doing anything in your own strength anymore.
So deep breath, and keep this in mind: the only person's reaction
you can control is your own, and the only one who can convict
is God. Be courageous, be calm, be kind, be *firm*.

I honestly can't remember what I said to Mark all those years
ago. I suspect I wasn't very calm, or kind at the time; but if I had
my time again I would say something like this:

> I know that porn is a part of our marriage, and
> I know you have repeatedly tried to stop, but
> I love you, and our marriage, too much to sit
> back and allow the poison of porn to destroy
> everything God has given us. Porn is not right.

Porn is not harmless. Your compulsion won't go away on its own and left unchecked will just get worse. My dearest wish is that we seek help together and restore the trust and intimacy that porn has stolen from us. But if you are not willing to do that, I will be seeking help alone, for me. I cannot force you to get the support and healing you need, but I will no longer allow your sin to hold me back from experiencing all that God has for me when I obey and trust Him. I will not turn a blind eye to this issue anymore, and I will not accept that there is nothing you can do about it. You can be free if you are willing to do whatever it takes.

Prepare for Resistance

Changing your behavior and putting up boundaries is most likely going to make your husband uncomfortable, and that's okay. Prepare yourself for the possibility of a variety of attempts to get you to relent, or soften your stance. But whatever comes your way, be it in the form of shaming accusations, angry threats, self-pitying moping, or tearful promises to change, hang on to the biblical promise that his pain and discomfort are necessary for change. Godly sorrow leads to repentance (2 Cor. 7:8–11).

You may also encounter resistance from unexpected quarters: your church, relatives, friends, or counselors. But, remember, any advice that has you doing anything other than putting up strong boundaries—no matter how "Christian" it is made to sound—is actually enabling the hook of addiction to sink in further. The Word of God commands women to be pure, which means standing firm against porn in their marriages, families, and homes.

Can't God Use Someone Else?

I have a special affinity for Bible stories where people try to wriggle out of doing what God is asking of them. From Gideon hiding in the threshing barn, to Moses' fear of public speaking, to Jonah hot-footing it to Tarshish, it is so comforting to see the humanity of man saying, "Thanks for the vote of confidence, Lord, but I think I'll pass on this one."

I wish I could say that God only uses those who are enthusiastic and feeling up to the job, but that's not the way He rolls. You do not get to choose whether or not God will use you to heal your husband; however, you do get a say in when it might happen. When Jonah jumped on a ship headed in the opposite direction to Nineveh, God sent him a storm, then a whale. Try as he may, Jonah could not avoid the good works that God had ordained for him. It is the same with you. You have the same choice: Go in the right direction now, or wait for your whale.

Out of obedience, you can choose to intentionally put a boundary up right now, or wait for your pain to get so intense that you have no choice but to issue a desperate ultimatum. Either way, God will use you as a catalyst to bring your husband to repentance. And remember—it's *God* bringing your husband to repentance, not you. The pressure and weight of changing a man on the heart level is something you could never do. God simply uses your visible and firm allegiance to Him as a tool in the process.

Still unconvinced? Take heart. Your human flesh is always going to fight undertaking a preemptive strike of this nature. Even though we are promised trials, tribulations, and persecution this side of heaven, who wants to provoke tension in their marriage if they don't have to? Who wants to feel distant from their spouse? Who needs that stress? Drawing a line in the sand on porn is not only a step of obedience, it's also a massive step of faith.

For those of you in a relationship where things are calm at the moment, and for whom tackling the issue of porn is going to cause serious waves, I encourage you to seek the Lord, and pray for wisdom and strength, asking Him to convict you to move when the time is right.

And for those of you who are exhausted and done trying to fight this on your own, I say to you: lay down your burden. Go on, lay it down. Cease your striving. Repent of trying to control your husband, or bring him to repentance in your own strength or strategy, and turn back to Christ.

Obey God.

Trust God.

Side with God.

He is your rock, your fortress, and your deliverer. Follow His Word, do not waver from His commands, and let Him fight this battle for you.

♥ ♥ ♥

The Truth about Recovery

B efore we get into the nuts and bolts of recovery, it is worth spending a little time looking at the bigger picture to help you understand where you are going and why.

Starting out in the Right Direction

You wouldn't climb aboard a ship without having a pretty good idea where it was heading. But in recovery, this is exactly what many people do. When couples are in crisis, they tend to reach out to any rescue boat that offers assistance. The problem with this is that not all boats are going to the same destination.

You have rafts of survivors, helpfully keeping each other out of the water but not making much forward progress. Then you have small dinghies manned by kind and well-meaning hobby-sailors, who, with all the best intentions in the world, can't take you through the rough seas ahead. Expensive cruise liners will get you where you need to be in a matter of months but may be beyond your budget. And finally, you have sturdy, tall ships, with an experienced crew who will let you hitch a ride while they teach you how they sail across the ocean. Unless you can afford a cruise liner, wait for a tall ship.

When my husband and I were in the market for a recovery program, my attitude was very much "this is your problem, you deal with it." There was no way I was going out of my way to help him sort out his mess, not after everything he had done.

At the time, I didn't understand how crucial it was for a wife to be actively involved at this stage. How could I? I had no idea that his addiction to porn was making it hard for him to be a good judge of anything. My husband stumbling into a healthy recovery group was due entirely to the grace of God.

Not everyone gets so lucky. Many couples waste years on unsuccessful therapy or groups. So, remember, when your husband is deep in his addiction, someone has to act as a surrogate pre-frontal cortex and make good decisions for him. Until you find a good therapist or program or group to take on that role, it is up to you.

Also, this bears saying: *your job is not to cure your husband, but to get him to someone who can.*

When assessing a recovery group, it is important to find out if they expect their members to get free and stay free. I know this sounds obvious, but a group is only as sober as its leaders. Just because your husband says he is attending a recovery group does not mean he is in recovery. Recovery is much more than just a sympathetic ear or a group of people that are stumbling all the time and okay with it. Too many wives learn this the hard way.

> *We must have spent thousands of dollars over a period of ten years trying to fix our marriage. He's seen two different counselors about his porn use, but every time he just switches on the charm and nothing changes. No one ever sees what he's really like. I thought things might get better when he started going to an accountability group at church. Sadly, two years later, the only thing that has changed is my heart. I don't think I can take much more of this.* (Sarah, age 54)

So How Can You Identify a Good Recovery Program?

It's actually very simple. The one key component you are looking for is rigorous honesty. Only consider programs where addicts are required to tell one hundred percent of the truth: past, present, and going forward. Unfortunately, not all programs require this level of honesty. Truth is tricky to enforce and addicts are masters of deception. Only therapists trained in porn addiction, or other addicts with a good period of sobriety, will be able to cut through the denial and the lies.

If your husband is not compelled to tell one hundred percent of the truth, it is unlikely he will get one hundred percent free.

The Truth and Nothing but the Truth

Why is telling the truth so important?

This may or may not come as a surprise, but beneath an addict's compulsive porn use lies a deeper issue of avoiding intimacy. In simple terms, there is an unmet need for connection that is driving the need for porn, or affairs, or anonymous sex. Now, don't misunderstand me, I'm not saying that his need for connection is because you have failed in some way. No, this lack has nothing to do with you. This started way before he met you. What I'm talking about is the way that he feels permanently disconnected from other people because he is primarily disconnected from the Lord—the ultimate source of connection his soul longs for—leading him to hide part of himself from God as well as others. Somewhere along the line he decided that expressing vulnerability and weakness was a bad idea, and he has been repressing those feelings ever since. Trouble is, hiding and repressing emotions always comes out sideways. Porn is a perfect outlet for feelings such as fear, anger, and powerlessness that come with being isolated from both God and people.

I am not telling you this to let your husband off the hook—what he is doing is still sin—but understanding the way into addiction helps you understand the way out. In recovery, addicts learn how to meet their God-given craving for connection in a healthy way, through being intimate with real people instead of porn. Fellowship is the foundation of recovery.

So, here's a conundrum: how can a person who avoids intimacy have fellowship? The answer can be found in this beautiful biblical principle from 1 John 1:7.

> If we walk in the light as he himself is in the
> light, we have fellowship with one another, and
> the blood of Jesus his Son cleanses us from all
> sin. (1 John 1:7)

It is by walking in the light—telling the truth to both God and other people—that we have fellowship. The reason this is healing is because Jesus is the light. Jesus is the power that breaks strongholds. When a man is brutally truthful about his behaviors, thoughts, and motives, he experiences the love and grace of God through other people. After sharing his deepest secrets, and darkest thoughts, he discovers that people still respect him and accept him. For the first time, he tastes the sweet freedom and joy of being both fully known and fully loved.

Why is telling the truth so difficult?

The recipe for recovery sounds so simple, doesn't it? Just four little words.

Tell the whole truth.

Should be plain sailing, right? And yet, it turns out that shining the light on who we really are is even more excruciating than confessing to all the shameful things we have done. Seriously, who wants to see themselves clearly?

Certainly not me. I would much rather go on believing that I don't have anger issues—that I only shout at my kids because they don't listen. Nor do I wish to examine my real motives behind my habit of unfriending the Facebookers who post photos of their perfect houses, high-achieving kids, and amazing vacations. And do not make me face the possibility that I may be a wee bit bitter—because some people in my life just don't deserve to be forgiven. Sounds reasonable, don't you think?

Ugh. Looking in the mirror is humbling. It's horribly hard to accept that I am broken, dysfunctional, and hopeless without God. It's tremendously difficult to admit that the problem isn't my circumstances or my kids or my lack—it's *me*. My flesh rebels against the notion that I am exactly the sort of sinner that Jesus came to save (even though my spirit rejoices).

It's hard to tell the truth because it is our very nature to hide. We avoid being 100 percent authentic and honest, even with ourselves. We can't help it. The very moment sin entered the garden of Eden, Adam and Eve jumped headfirst into the shrubbery—their instinct was to hide from God and deflect the blame. Instead of coming clean and begging for forgiveness, they attempted to fool their all-knowing, ever-present Creator. And we have been doing the same ever since.

Why do you have to tell the truth to other people?

Recovery from addiction is the process of relearning how to meet the need for connection through being intimate with real people rather than counterfeit substitutes. It's the bird going back to other real-life birds instead of neon cardboard cut-outs.

This is why group work is so important. If we are to prove ourselves "doers of the word, and not merely hearers who delude themselves" (James 1:22 NASB), it is not enough to confess to God alone in the privacy of the prayer closet, we need to be fully authentic and transparent with one other.

Walking fully in the light means being 100 percent truthful with each other. Ninety-nine percent of the truth is still a lie. The truth cannot be filtered or watered down. This is where many "recovery groups" forfeit true fellowship and true healing. They allow partial truth and don't insist on the entire truth. Members of the group who say "I had a tough week" are not compelled to describe in detail the nature and manifestation of their sin. This is how they fudge the truth, not only from others, but also from themselves. This explains why many men who have attended "recovery groups" for years simply don't get better.

As a wife, you can't ask the leader of the group the content of what is said during sessions; this is confidential. But you can ask if rigorous honesty is a requirement of participation. Find out what the leader's policy is on transparency between husband and wife. Does the group collude with secrets? Be bold. Ask the questions. A bit of polite, but judicious, probing could save you years of frustration and unnecessary misery.

And remember: a good group can literally save your marriage. It saved mine.

Groups are most effective when two things are happening. When those sharing are rigorously and brutally honest about everything they do and think, and when the other participants respond with grace and truth. As we learned in chapter 2, the brain of an addict is literally not thinking straight. Addicts need to be challenged on distorted thinking and unacceptable behavior—sometimes they know these things and are trying to side-step them, but other times they have legitimately lost touch with them and need someone with a clearer mind to help them readjust to what's normal, faithful, and right. This is fellowship in action.

As painful as it is, being confronted with the truth of who we are is the lynchpin of recovery. In the Bible we see King David brought to his knees by the truth of who he was. David had committed adultery with Bathsheba, and then had her husband murdered. However, it wasn't until the prophet Nathan told him a story about sheep that David actually repented. As the story goes, a man with plenty of sheep stole a sheep from another man who only had one. Through Nathan's confrontation, David realized that he was "that man," and his eyes were opened to the awful truth about himself. He was just as calloused and greedy as the heartless sheep-stealer. By his own mouth, David pronounced the sheep thief deserving of death. And by his own mouth in Psalm 51, he pronounced his own sinfulness. This was David's healing balm of truth.

Recovery can be a time of intense spiritual transformation.

I found my home among the sick and broken and experienced grace and fellowship like never before. Although it was a brutal and painful time, I am profoundly grateful to have been through it. It was only when I began to walk in the light and saw myself fully, that I truly grasped how desperately I need a Savior. By telling the whole truth, I relinquished control over my precious image and exposed all of my sin for others to see. But, instead of feeling judged and rejected, I felt known and accepted. (Paul, age 42)

Once the sweetness of authentic fellowship with God and others is tasted, it is hard to be satisfied with anything less.

Why do husbands have to tell their wives the whole truth?

You may have heard it said that there are some things a wife doesn't need to know. In a recent survey, 770 pastors were asked whether they would advise another pastor to share with his wife if he was struggling with porn. Only 58 percent thought it was a good idea.[1] The others were concerned that the truth would cause unnecessary strife in the marriage. And yet, the exact opposite is true. When porn use is kept secret, wives go crazy trying to work out what is going wrong with their marriages, often blaming themselves. I have yet to find one wife who is grateful that she has been "considerately" shielded from the truth for years.

It is deception, not the truth, that destroys marriages. The Bible offers zero passages sanctioning partial-confession, hiding a little bit of sin. Sure, discretion is something valued in the Bible, but not when it comes to sin. Sin doesn't call for discretion. It calls for full confession and full repentance, plain and simple.

As we discovered in chapter 1, the old adage of "what she doesn't know doesn't hurt her" is never true, not to mention unbiblical. <u>Wives always know something is wrong; they just don't always know exactly what it is.</u>

> *Every night I would have the same dream that my husband was having an affair even though I had absolutely no reason to suspect that this was true. Every morning I would wake up distressed and paranoid. When he finally told me that he was struggling with porn, it all made sense. I still felt angry and betrayed, but his willingness to be vulnerable and honest gave me hope for our future.* (Janelle, age 32)

Divorces do happen in recovery, but they happen when men refuse to get with the program and tell the truth, which inevitably leads them to slip back into using porn. Some men try every way they can to "heal" their marriage without committing to full disclosure to their wife. When faced with this requirement, more men quit at this stage than any other. And yet without the truth there is no hope for personal sobriety or relational reconciliation.

There is one caveat here. Although it is important that your husband confesses lustful thoughts if they begin to take up residence in his head, you are not the right choice for his accountability partner. This is what men in his group are for. In the emotionally turbulent times of early recovery, you cannot be there for him in this capacity. Not only may you find it triggering to hear his thoughts, you need headspace to be able to focus on your own healing.

Recovery for your husband is all about learning how to prevent thoughts from taking root by confessing quickly to his support network. This skill of automatic confession is key to standing strong in times of fierce temptation. This is how he builds up intimacy with other men. However, if your husband's thoughts cross over into action—for example, he goes out of his way to get a coworker's phone number, or to click on that image, that does need to be confessed to you. Exposing tempting thoughts to the light is part of good recovery; acting on them is not.

Further down the road, when your husband has a good period of sobriety and your marriage is in a much stronger place, you might consider being available to him, to pray with him, and for him, if he is being attacked by prolonged lustful thoughts. This is what Mark and I do now. But it took a long time to get there. I don't enjoy being reminded that my husband has a weakness in this area and will always need to be vigilant about it. However, because I have done a lot of healing myself, I am able to separate myself from his addiction and be there for him without getting triggered.

Why do wives have to tell the truth too?

When my husband began his recovery process, we were told that it would significantly speed up the process if I got onboard and entered my own recovery. This didn't make a lot of sense to me at the time. As far as I was concerned, and in my naiveté, I

assumed he was the only one with problems. However, I did the
math and decided that since the overall cost was discounted if we
both pursued recovery, it was worth giving it a go.

In recovery, I learned that wives of porn addicts develop
many ways of coping, all of which are variations of hiding their
truth: staying busy or staying aloof, being hyper-controlling, or
perhaps even hyper-sexual. Though I didn't know all these things
at the start, I eventually learned that recovery for me meant
getting off the merry-go-round and getting in touch with how
hurt and angry I really was. Yes, my husband was the one whose
sin created the mess we were in, but my ways of coping weren't
helping me, him, or my relationship with God.

Righteous anger is such an important part of the healing
process. It must never be rushed over through pressure to act
like a "good" wife who readily "forgives" without any real heart-
work involved. God was righteously angry with Israel when they
strayed. In Jeremiah 2:24 He likened them to donkeys in heat
sniffing in the wind. Porn use is infidelity. If we are going by
Jesus' definitions on sexual sin, it's *adultery* plain and simple, and
it is holy and right for a wife to be angry, just as God is angry
when we stray from our covenant with Him.

Another big part of being truthful for me meant acknowledging my sorrow and grief. The husband I thought I married
never really existed, and the marriage I thought I had was a lie.
My loss needed to be grieved before something new could be
reborn.

Telling my husband the truth about my anger and grief was
important for us both. I needed to see that my husband could

not just "handle" my emotions, but understand them as normal and right responses to covenant-breaking. I needed to know he could hear my heart with all its emotions and empathize with me, while still remaining engaged. It was me revealing how I was really doing inside that finally pulled us back together.

Without truth there is no hope.

With truth there is endless hope.

My husband is not the man I thought I had married. He is so much more. Praise the Lord! I feel closer to him than ever. We tell each other everything now—the good, the bad and the ugly. It turns out that I did make a good choice all those years ago.

So, now that you have a clearer understanding of the direction you need to be heading, climb aboard and let's learn how to sail this ship.

CHAPTER 5

♥   ♥   ♥

The Tools of Recovery

A few months ago, my six-year-old had elective eye surgery for a wandering eye that was below the visible spectrum. In other words, nobody ever noticed it. A week before the surgery, Mark and I—neither of us sleeping much—looked at each other and said, "Why are we doing this?" At our next appointment the doctor patiently explained how our son's vision was only going to get worse and how it would impact his life later. The earlier we undertook medical intervention to straighten the eye, she said, the easier it would be for his brain to rewire. We simply had to trust her. She had been doing this for thirty years and had helped hundreds of children.

Goodness! We tried, but we're talking *eyeballs* here. As in a person's permanent vision for the entirety of life.

In the interest of honesty, I've got to say the whole process was pretty brutal. Not for the little'un; he bounced back as fast as Dash from *The Incredibles*. My husband and I, not quite so fast.

After the surgery, my son looked 100 percent worse—so red raw and cross-eyed that he wouldn't have been out of place in a *Tom and Jerry* cartoon. What in heaven's name had we done?! I clung to the doctor's pre-op warnings: "He's going to be crossed-eyed for a while, but this is actually a good sign. Prepare yourself. It's going to look like it's getting worse before it gets better."

Here's my point. Understanding why we were putting our little boy, and ourselves, through this experience didn't remove our fear or make the operation less painful; but it did enable us to push through those challenging early days after the surgery without completely losing it. It helped us keep the ordeal in perspective and focus on the desired outcome. In short, we had hope.

Nothing I say can entirely remove your apprehension about tackling the issue of porn in your marriage. I wish there were a way to make this process pain-free, but there isn't. What I can do is reassure you that you are doing the right thing and prepare you for the bumps ahead. By giving you realistic expectations of what recovery looks like, I can offer you hope. In this chapter we will cover the four main tools used in the early stages of recovery:

- Disclosure
- Partner Survey
- Safety Plan
- Celibacy

Understanding why you are undertaking each of these challenging steps will help you set off in the right direction and stay on the narrow path.

Tool #1: Disclosure

In the previous chapter we talked about the importance of walking 100 percent in the light as based on 1 John 1:7. The first way to ensure you're following this biblical command in your recovery process is by doing a formal disclosure; this is a crucial step. Disclosure is a mutual, planned, facilitated event where your husband reads a document he has prepared to you that contains the whole truth regarding his sexual sin. If the thought of a full disclosure feels overwhelming to you, rest assured you are not alone. Disclosure is daunting for literally everyone. Think of it as the therapeutic equivalent of sterilizing a wound—excruciating, but utterly necessary. When you are trying to prevent infection from setting in, you have to get *all* the dirt out.

Elements disclosed may include the following:

- What types of porn he has viewed, approximate time frames, and frequency
- An estimate of the total number of hours he has spent viewing it over his lifetime
- Other types of sexual acting out, approximate time frames, and frequency
- Number of sexual partners he has acted out with in real life (including the names of those known to you)
- The date of last contact with any affair partners, and the date of last acting out with them

- Estimate of amount of money spent and where the money has come from
- Health issues, such as the risk of sexually transmitted diseases
- Incidents that may have directly or indirectly impacted your children (including exposure to porn or affair partners)
- Brief sexual autobiography. You will typically be asked whether you want to hear a complete history or start at the beginning of their relationship. (Most wives want to hear a complete history for the sake of understanding lifelong patterns they may not have previously known about.)

Breaking the stronghold of pornography requires dragging every secret into the light. Addiction is built on secrecy and isolation, and where secrets remain, toxic shame breeds. For your husband to stand any hope of staying sober—and yes, being free from porn for him will be the equivalent of sobriety—he has to get every single shameful incident out. Although a difficult and painful process, the day of disclosure is often a pivotal moment for the marriage. Your husband's willingness to tell the whole truth will provide that critical foundation for the restoration of trust. It gives a starting place where you can both look back and say, "Here was the moment we decided there was no more secrets, no more sins hidden in the dark, and no more lies. This was the day it all came out, and the full extent of what we were dealing with was laid bare."

A Few Words of Caution

Disclosure is not recommended if either of you has initiated divorce proceedings. Neither should it be attempted without the supervision of an experienced third party. Not only will you be putting yourself in a potentially unstable situation, but it is unlikely that you will get a full and thorough disclosure.

> Our pastor advised us to do a disclosure on our own, just the two of us. My husband gave vague blanket statements to the questions I asked, and I ended up feeling frustrated, hopeless, and demoralized. We would never get to the truth. (Shelley)

When therapists work with clients on disclosure, they go back and forth several times to ensure that the document is thorough and specific and strictly factual.

What is NOT included in a disclosure are the following elements:

- Graphic details of sexual behaviors
- Names of sexual partners not known to you
- Locations of acting out, other than your home
- Thoughts or feelings about acting-out partners
- Fantasies or thought life

"She'll leave me if I tell the truth."

A common fear that men have before disclosure is that their wife will leave them once they hear the whole story. While it is understandable to be worried about the future, the only long-term way to save the marriage is to address the root problem. Focusing on avoiding divorce at any cost, especially when that involves further deliberate deception, is doomed to fail. Recovery is a process of surrender, of faith. By agreeing to do a full disclosure your husband is putting his marriage on the altar and saying to God, "Your will, not mine, be done." And the reality is, when husbands obey God and tell the entire truth—and continue to tell the truth—divorce rarely happens, even in cases where the acting out has been extensive. God is able to work miracles in a wife's heart to forgive a God-fearing and repentant husband.

Far more detrimental than full disclosure are attempts at damage control. When a husband fearfully holds back part of the truth, it always makes things worse. Any form of staggered disclosure, where partial truths are revealed incrementally, is agonizing for his wife. Trust is shattered as she loses any sense of being able to trust her feelings and intuition.

> If I could say one thing to husbands, it would be to please have enough courage and respect to get it all out the first time. My husband nearly killed me by dragging it out. I had to endure three disclosures, each one revealing yet more acting out. I can't tell you how much it hurt. Just get it all out;

then it's over. Telling it bit by bit makes it so much worse. (Shelley)

A husband who is willing to do a full disclosure is a husband who wants to get better. Notice I say *willing*, not *wanting*. Your husband doesn't have to be enthusiastic about this process; he just has to do it. Recovery is all about taking contrary actions: making a call when you want to isolate yourself; attending a recovery group meeting at the end of a long day; doing a disclosure when you just want to leave your past in the past. I get it. It's hard to see how dredging stuff up from the past—stuff that happened way before you even met—might benefit your relationship now. But it is worth it. Indeed, once the aftershock of disclosure has subsided and the process of rebuilding trust has begun, the overwhelming majority of people (96 percent of addicts and 93 percent of partners of addicts) come to view disclosure as a vital part of their recovery.[1]

Disclosure validated all my fears and worries and gave me a clear head. I remember feeling immense relief. I wasn't the crazy one. Not that he was, but I wasn't crazy for all the red flags I saw but he denied. (Mandy)

From that point forward things fell into place, and I felt like I could breathe. Once I knew everything that we were dealing with, there was a chance that things could get better. (Christy)

But what do you do if your instincts are telling you that you still have not been given the whole truth? That he is still hiding something? If there has been a lot of deception and mind games in your marriage, to doubt complete disclosure is understandable. At this point, I am going to tell you something that may shock you. It is the practice of many professionally trained counselors to incorporate various methods that address the pressing question, "How do I know my husband is telling the complete truth?" For certainty is a difficult issue. What's more, this is where counselors, and their patients, may disagree. Some couples believe that "faith" or "trust" should be guarded at all costs by not using tools to "scientifically" verify whether or not the truth has been told. Others, mutually, will decide that an empirical approach would greatly help them move on after disclosure. And so, under the supervision of trained professionals, they utilize a polygraph test.

I know, now you're thinking, *Are you kidding me? That's like something out of a movie.* Most people respond that way initially. And, sure, it may not be for everybody. But, regardless of your position, it is one way to address the issue of certainty.

As I'm sure you already know, a polygraph is a lie-detector machine that works by detecting changes in physiological characteristics, such as a person's pulse and breathing rates. Polygraph exams are frequently used to draw a line under disclosure, helping a wife feel confident that her husband has finally told the truth. You'd be surprised how often they are undertaken in these cases. But when you consider that a heavy user of porn has had their brain rewired and their judgment seriously compromised, employing a polygraph begins to seem less like science fiction and more like simple common sense. According to my husband, approximately 50 percent of his clients choose to go down this route.

Yes, I know it's depressing to realize that your marriage has come to this. Every wife wants to believe that her husband will tell the whole truth because he is doing so *before God*, not a machine. After all, God knows the accuracy of his sin far better than any lie detector. But again, you have to remember that an addict's reality is seriously warped, and that includes his spirituality. Absolutely, your husband *should* fear God more than a lie detector—but that's like expecting a drug addict to think clearly about his words before the Lord while under the influence. Honesty with the Lord and healthy fear of God will come as an addict detoxes. But in a compromised state with an inebriated view of reality, sometimes the best starting place for a baseline is a polygraph.

> It was hard to go down the polygraph route. I really struggled and prayed about it. Do I have good enough reasons to want this? But in my heart of hearts I knew that I did need proof. At first my husband got angry, but then he started dumping more information. By the time of the polygraph, I felt confident it was all out, but I'm not sure we would have gotten there without the polygraph. (Christy)

When to Have a Disclosure

When it comes to the timing of a disclosure, there are two options. Some practitioners work with clients for months to prepare the disclosure document, and others offer an intensive format over three to four days. There are benefits to both approaches.

Taking time to work with a therapist for a few months before disclosure may lessen the potential for omissions and help your husband gain insight into his behavior. Yet many wives feel that for their own mental health and the safety of their family, this isn't a realistic option. They feel like they need to know the extent of what they are dealing with *now*. When my husband agrees to work with a couple, he requires that a full disclosure is undertaken fairly quickly. In his opinion, by the time couples come to see him, continuing with the deception by postponing disclosure normally poses more of a threat to the relationship than does telling the truth.

> *I just needed to know the truth. What bothered me more than what my husband had done was the fact he deceived me for the entirety of our relationship. This was the hardest thing to face. Plus, I had this feeling in the back of my mind—a fear that everything would still not come out—and I needed that to stop. Even though I was scared to find out what I might be dealing with, I was also encouraged because I knew that we were finally going to dump all the dirt on the table.* (Christy)

How to Prepare for Disclosure

It is totally normal to be daunted by the prospect of hearing a full disclosure. Every wife I've talked to about this described fear and anxiety caused by a runaway imagination.

> *The unknown was scary to me. My imagination was going wild, and I couldn't help going down dark places. My big fear was that there would be something on there that I couldn't live with or forgive.* (Miriam)

> *On one hand I felt confident that I knew everything, but there was this lingering fear that there was more, and I was scared of what it could be. My mind would race off to really unhealthy places and imagine horrible things.* (Mandy)

> *It was so daunting. I had no idea how high the cliff was that I was about to fall off.* (Shelley)

Here are six steps you can take to prepare yourself for a disclosure:

1. Talk to a wife in recovery. I know it is scary to reach out to a stranger, but nothing is going to reassure you more than making a connection to someone who has already gone through what you are facing. When everything else in your life seems unreal and spinning out of control, that person acts as your anchor, making you feel less alone and disorientated in your newfound reality. And, unlike friends and family, you will not have to manage her fears and expectations for your future. You can simply vent. Often, finding another woman in recovery is not easy, so my husband will offer a mentor to both the wife and the husband during their first session with him.

I remember where I was in my house when I made that first call. I was curled on the floor by the piano. I was scared to make the call, but I needed to make the call. So I did. It was a big scary healthy dose of reality. I felt like the wife I called had run fifteen miles, and I hadn't even started. But then she said these words: 'I'll be here for you. It's going to be really hard, but I've been there and I'll be here for you. Call me.' Knowing she was there made all the difference. (Shelley)

I think I would have lost my ever-loving mind if I couldn't call my mentor. I would go sit in my car in my garage and talk to her because my kids or my husband were in the house, and I would just sob on the phone. It was really helpful to be able to spew what emotion was going on in my heart and brain at that moment. I knew she wasn't going to freak out, and at the end of the conversation she would help me figure out what to do. Up to this point I had only talked to male pastors and counselors who would logically try to help me, but sometimes I just needed to cry. (Christy)

2. Prepare questions beforehand. If your counselor does not have a formal disclosure preparation form, take the time to think through what sort of detail you need and don't need to hear. Communicate this to your counselor before the day of disclosure.

3. Make a transportation plan for afterwards. I strongly urge you to drive in separate cars or to arrange for one of you to get a lift after the disclosure. The last place you are going to want to be is stuck in a car on a long journey with your husband. You will need time to decompress on your own.

4. Clear your schedule ahead of time. As you don't know how you are going to feel for the first few days after disclosure, it's a good idea to plan for some breathing room. Think through what commitments are going to make you feel pressure to "be on" and reschedule or cancel.

5. Plan to call your support network. Arrange a call for immediately afterwards to debrief with someone you trust, who can simply hear you and empathize with your feelings.

6. Pray without ceasing. Make no mistake, recovery is a spiritual dogfight. Undertaking a full disclosure puts you squarely in enemy territory. This is where you start taking back ground and breaking those demonic strongholds. In your prayer time, confess your fear and your runaway imagination, and pray for supernatural strength and protection. One way I prepare myself for battle—especially on tough days when I know the fiery darts of the Enemy will be coming at me thick and fast—is to have Scripture locked and loaded in my mind, on my fridge, in my car, in my purse, by the sink, sometimes even on the back of my hand. I know it sounds cliché, but when you are fighting this hard, being constantly reminded of the truth really does help. As you spend time in the Word, ask God to give you battle verses just for you.

Here's a couple of mine:

> I will keep my eyes always on the Lord. With him at my right hand, I will not be shaken. (Ps. 16:8 niv)

> You will keep in perfect peace all who trust in you, all whose thoughts are fixed on you. (Isa. 26:3 nlt)

Disclosure Day

Disclosure day is ground zero. Nothing will ever be quite the same again. Shining such a powerful spotlight on your marriage is blinding and disorienting, but it will enable you to find your way back to the path. While you and your husband are aware that somehow you've strayed off the path of a healthy marriage, you won't know exactly how far until disclosure day. You could be two feet from it or you could be lost miles away in the woods. It's scary to imagine how far you could be. But, let me assure you it's far worse to *not* know and simply assume you'll find the way back eventually, because you most likely won't. This is why this step is so important. Disclosure orients you with the full facts of where you stand so you can stop blindly wandering around and start making your way back to the path.

> *During the disclosure I felt shocked, ashamed, sad, and mad. But I do remember that toward the end I actually felt empathy for my husband. I was truly heartbroken for him. For everything he'd been exposed to. How he'd made the decision to go down this path.*
>
> *I liked how my therapist kept checking in on me to make sure I was okay during the disclosure. Even though it was horrendous, I felt engulfed in protection. Someone was there, taking care of me. There was someone there to tend to my stab wounds as they happened. Weirdly, it felt safe. I felt that my husband could then tell me the whole truth and that I could be honest and true about how I was feeling in the moment.*
>
> *Afterward I was numb, shocked, dumbfounded. I just wanted to be quiet and sit. It wasn't until weeks later that other feelings of anger, sadness, and bitterness emerged.*
>
> *It has been over four years now, and I'm mostly grateful that we went through the experience. I still feel a little sad, now that everything is out; but I couldn't imagine our marriage any different without a full*

disclosure. It has enabled me to be totally honest with him. Now we are walking together, hand-in-hand, toward something beautiful, instead of further apart as when there were secrets between us. (Miriam)

Tool #2: Partner Response Survey

As I've mentioned before, it is not just husbands who need to walk in the light. Real fellowship in a marriage requires you to tell the truth also. Be prepared to dig deep and get in touch with how you really feel. The Partner Response Survey helps you identify ways that your husband's compulsive porn use has affected you mentally, physically, sexually, and spiritually. In a supervised session, you read your answers aloud, and your husband is not permitted to respond or defend himself. He simply has to hear you. Without name-calling or blaming, you express your hurt, pain, frustration, anger, and disgust without fear of contradiction or reprisal.

Some wives find this process cathartic and validating—a chance to vomit out all their toxic emotions and finally be heard. For others, coming out of denial is painful, like the ripping off of an enormous Band-Aid right across their heart.

I thought doing the partner survey would be easy. I thought I was connected. But when I actually sat down and began going through the questions, I realized that it had been much worse than I thought. I had buried so much. But when I stopped and thought about all the incidents cumulatively, it was overwhelming. His porn had affected me far more seriously for far longer than I thought. I was not okay. I had not been okay for a long time. What started out as an exercise to connect my husband to my pain actually connected me back to my heart. My broken bleeding heart. (Christy)

Hearing your pain and anger expressed in a healthy way will be an important aspect of healing for you, of course, but also your husband. Remember that addiction callouses the heart and impairs the ability to be empathetic. God can use your full disclosure to help your husband not just understand the error of his ways on an informational level, but really *feel* it. Though he may be defensive or angry at first, seeing the real hurt and consequences for his sin is important.

I wasn't sure how he was going to react. I cried through most of my survey. It was a lot harder than I thought. My husband was quiet, but I could tell he was getting angry. Afterwards, it was a little tense for several days, and he remained angry in our counseling sessions. Then one night when we were driving home after a counseling session, he took my hand and put it on his face. There were tears coming down his face. My husband is not a crier. I have never seen him cry unless it was at a funeral or when one of our kids was being born. He cried the entire rest of the way home and neither of us said a word. That was the moment when my husband finally broke. From that point on, things were still hard, but things were better. (Christy)

Recovery is about so much more than just getting sober from porn; it is about learning how to be vulnerable and truly intimate with each other. The Partner Response Survey helps you have a hard, honest conversation. The next step will be for your husband to reach out and connect with you in your pain and not get defensive. In recovery he will learn how to say, "I hear that you are angry with me, and your anger makes sense to me," or "I hear that you are disgusted. Can you tell me more about that?" It's at this point that healing really starts. Both his and yours. Although you will still be mad at him and probably won't trust him, it will help you start to feel connected to him. Subconsciously, over time, you may even begin to see him as a friend you can be honest with, someone you might consider trusting your heart with again. This is how genuine confession and repentance works.

Tool #3: Celibacy

Against the typical advice you may get from a friend or well-meaning counselor, a period of celibacy is highly recommended at the beginning of recovery. Having more sex is not the answer, especially in the weeks following a full disclosure. Your husband's altered expectations around sex need time to reboot, as does his warped view of reality. The suggested time frame for celibacy is normally ninety days. This provides time for husbands to "dry out."

You're probably familiar with the concept of detox or "drying out" in relation to drugs or alcohol, but you may not be aware that it also applies to porn. Drying out from porn is a difficult and gradual process. You can't just pour your secret stash down the sink and be done with it. It's stuck inside your head, available to get you high at any time.

But your husband is not the only one who will benefit from a break from sex. Recovery also means reclaiming those aspects of *your* own sexuality that have been impacted and damaged by his addiction. Taking time out to heal your sexual wounds is critical. Ninety days is the recommended guideline, not a rule. There is no pressure to resume having sex if you are not ready. The following symptoms are commonly reported by wives of porn/sex addicts:

- Avoidance, fear or lack of interest in sex
- Viewing sex as an obligation
- Negative feelings like anger, disgust, or guilt whenever touched
- Difficulties becoming aroused
- Feeling dirty and contaminated
- Feeling emotionally distant, and not able to be present, during sex

- Intrusive or disturbing thoughts about what your husband has been viewing/doing
- Pain during sex
- Increased insecurity about physical attractiveness[2]

A period of celibacy also gives you head space to reflect on the rest of your relationship.

> *During our time of celibacy, I learned that I used sex to feel close to my husband and to feel loved. I didn't know how to be intimate and vulnerable without using sex. I was SUPER surprised by that. I remember Googling "How to be intimate with my husband without sex." After two months, we really started to talk and share and get to know one another. Sometimes I wish we did periods of celibacy more often. Maybe not ninety days though.* (Mandy)

While some wives are overjoyed and relieved at the prospect of an enforced time of celibacy, others are more resistant. If sex is the only time you feel connected to your husband, the thought of having to go without that comfort is scary. It is also hard for some wives to overcome the voices in their head telling them that they shouldn't deny their husbands. The lies swirl incessantly.

You can't expect a man to hang around if you aren't satisfying him.

It's your job to help him resist porn.

If you don't have sex with him, he'll probably relapse.

Let me be clear: None of these thoughts are true.

Now, please don't misunderstand me. I'm not saying wives shouldn't want to have sex with their husbands. Far from it. It is God-honoring to love your husband in a myriad of ways, with all the regularity and passion you can. Longing for sexual intimacy with your husband is healthy and godly. However, using sex to escape your reality or doing it begrudgingly out of fear or obligation is not.

And if things have gotten so bad that you couldn't care less if you never had sex with your husband again, remember, God hasn't given up on your sex life. He desires your sexual wholeness and fulfillment just as much as He desires your husband's. I would even go so far as to say it grieves and angers Him to see how your sexual life—your sexual psychology and your sexual functioning—has been impacted and wounded by your husband's porn addiction. The point of recovery is not simply to heal his brokenness, but to restore you *both*, fully. This is another reason why bringing women into the discussion about porn addiction in churches is so important. In order to help couples move from sexual brokenness into sexual wholeness, the church is going to have to get over its squeamishness about talking about porn, *and* female sexuality the way God intended it.

> For twenty years I had disconnected sex with my husband, not realizing I was having disconnected sex. Now sex is totally different. If we try to have sex, and one of us is not connected, we just have to stop,

because it isn't going to work anymore. We can't do what we previously did because we now realize there is a difference. (Christy)

The power of celibacy is nothing new. In 1 Corinthians 7:5 (NET), Paul says "Do not deprive each other, except by mutual agreement for a specified time, so that you may devote yourselves to prayer." Celibacy is a powerful time of transformation. In many of the interviews I conducted, there was a common thread. *"Ninety days sucks, but boy, oh boy, sex after ninety days is a whole different experience."* Celibacy provides both of you with the time and space to disengage from unhealthy sexual expression and discover God's design for your sex life.

I was so apprehensive about celibacy, but now I'm on the other side. I'm a huge proponent. If we had not done it, I don't know if my husband would have ever gotten better. We were using sex for all kinds of stuff. We weren't connected emotionally. It was only after sex that we felt okay. Sometimes we would have fights and then have sex. I had sexual issues from my past and so did he. Both of us were using sex as a tool for something it was not intended to be.

I think I needed the ninety days of celibacy as much as my husband did. It made us totally reevaluate how we were connecting and how we showed love to one another. It was a totally different experience to the one I thought it was going to be.

I remember our miracle moment. We were sitting on the floor in our bedroom, talking about something to do with therapy. I had been crying and was really upset. My husband looked at me and started to ask me all these questions about how I felt about different things that had happened in our marriage. At first, I was reluctant to tell him because I thought it was a trap. I thought I would say something and he would throw it all back in my face. But he kept asking how I felt and telling me that he understood and that these things must have been really hard for me. He was empathizing and sympathizing with me in a way that he had never done before. By now I was sobbing. Real ugly crying. Snot everywhere. And I remember looking at him and thinking I'm really turned on by you now and really attracted to you. And he said that he was too to me. We sat there looking at each other having this moment of connection that we had never had before. We weren't having sex. We weren't doing anything we weren't supposed to be doing. I thought, Oh, this is it! This is what we were supposed

*to be experiencing all along and we've
never had this happen before.* (Christy)

Having said all that, I am well aware that just reading about the topic of sex is enough to make many wives feel anxious. For many painful reasons sex has always been a minefield, even before they found themselves married to a porn addict. This aversion to anything sexual is a much deeper issue, going way back. This is a different issue from the aversion that wives typically and understandably feel as a result of their husband's porn use. A husband filling his mind full of pornographic images of other women is going to pour cold water on any wife's libido. However, for some women, even the thought of sex holds terror or great fear for them. Forcing themselves to be intimate with their husband has always felt like it had dire internal consequences—like there is a giant invisible barrier that needs to be overcome, every time.

Here's a term you may not have heard before, but it is one that I want to bring to your attention. Coined by Dr. Patrick Carnes, a leading expert and author on sexual addiction, *sexual anorexia* describes a compulsive avoidance of sex. He puts it like this:

> Sexual anorexia is an obsessive state in which the physical, mental, and emotional task of avoiding sex dominates one's life. Like self-starvation with food or compulsive debting or hoarding with money, deprivation with sex can make one feel powerful and defended against all hurts.[3]

The reason I am including this information is because it is not uncommon for a woman who is sexually anorexic to be unconsciously drawn to a man who is sexually compulsive, and vice versa. They are the perfect dysfunctional fit. Each condition locks the other in denial. Wives can blame their lack of interest on their husband's acting out. Husbands can blame their acting out on their wife's lack of interest. However, when one starts to get healthy, the other is forced to face their own distorted reality. Oftentimes the healing of a husband's porn addiction can lead to the uncovering and healing of a wife's sexual anorexia. You see, God's plan for recovery isn't just about removing porn from your marriage, it's about totally transforming your entire lives. And that may include sexual wholeness beyond what you ever imagined or thought possible.

So it is with the greatest gentleness I say take heart, dear reader; if this is your particular struggle, there is hope. The healing path out of sexual anorexia into sexual wholeness is neither quick nor easy, but it is possible.

I have a fierce heart for women battling this alone, especially when teachings on marriage tend to focus on how important sex is to husbands without even giving a moment's pause to consider wives who might be suffering from sexual anorexia. For wives who desperately want to make their husband happy sexually, but experience overwhelming fear and anxiety every time they try, messages like these only leave them feeling more hopeless, ashamed, and desperate than before. Sexual anorexia is a real, debilitating condition, just like porn addiction is a real, debilitating condition. Women (and men) who compulsively avoid sex need to be validated in their pain, strengthened in their faith, and encouraged to reach out for help just as much as people who struggle with porn. Both are intimacy disorders. They are simply different sides of the same coin. Both desperately need to hear that freedom from all types of sexual brokenness is possible in Christ.

Tool #4: Safety Plan

There's a reason cabin crews recite a safety script at the start of every flight. By the time the plane starts plummeting, it's too late to issue instructions. Nobody's listening. In recovery it is the same. You have to prepare for unexpected patches of extreme turbulence before they happen. The time to think about what to do if your husband relapses is not after the event, but before. A safety plan is a personalized, practical plan of what to do if your husband looks at porn again. The point of the safety plan is not to punish him but to help you respond in a healthy and effective way.

Every safety plan is different. Wives need different things to feel safe. Completing the safety plan requires you to think through how you would feel if your husband slipped and what you would need in order to feel safe. Do you need him to sleep in another room for a while? Do you need him to leave the house for a few days? Do you need to schedule an hour when he hears how this has affected you?

> Initially I didn't want a safety plan. I didn't want to have to have consequences. It felt like a contract. It felt wrong, I thought it would traumatize our kids and would be a

punishment for me if I had to implement it.
It took a while for me to understand that if
I want to have healthy boundaries, this was
the avenue to start this process.

I needed a lot of help to fill the plan out.
I didn't know what I could even expect from
my husband and I didn't trust myself to
make appropriate consequences. (Shelley)

At first glance, asking your husband to leave the house for a while or refusing to have sex for a certain number of days may appear controlling and punitive, but here's the truth. Without some sort of enforced emotional or physical distance, it is difficult to disengage from the craziness that accompanies a "slip" and take care of your own needs without some sort of enforced emotional or physical distance. When emotions run high, it is too easy to get pulled back into old dysfunctional ways of relating. Just think of the ways you slip back into old family patterns when you go home for the holidays. When family chaos starts to escalate, everyone starts acting like their eighteen-year-old selves. The same is true for marital chaos, especially in the case of porn relapse. We all go back to our old selves when we feel freshly hurt or betrayed.

Although absolutely understandable, trying to get your husband to see how much he has hurt you through tears or angry recriminations will have little effect. A healthy response means calmly detaching from the situation, reaching out for your own support, asking your husband to do the same, and taking all the time and space you need to process through this latest betrayal.

*The safety plan was super helpful in the
beginning when I didn't know how to
work the program or what steps to take.
Previously I had spent all my energy trying
to control my husband, and it never worked.
Now I didn't need to. I liked knowing that I
had something in my back pocket if things
went wrong. It helped me stay clear-minded
when things got crazy.* (Mandy)

Separating yourself from your husband is also healing for
him. It enables him to feel the natural consequences of betraying
you (and your kids if you have them). These consequences are
an essential part of breaking his denial that his sin and acting
out doesn't hurt anyone else. He likely got away with years of sin
without any natural consequences apart from what was happening in his brain. The consequences were happening on the inside
for him, but not in his outer relationships. He did not go through
the natural separation that happens between people when trust
is breached, so having to experience them now is vital. A safety
plan redefines "normal" for him (and you). Sin *should* have relational consequences, and both of you abiding by the safety plan
allows that "should" to become reality. It helps your husband
experientially understand Romans 6:23—that the wages of his
sins, slips, and actions really are relational death between himself
and others (and God!).

*Asking my husband to pack his stuff and
leave was one of the hardest things I have*

ever done, but it was a pivotal moment.
That was the last time he slipped. (Christy)

The time frame for your husband to confess to any acting out is clearly stated in the safety plan (normally within twelve hours). Sticking to this time frame is important, and extra consequences for non-compliance are built in. These provisions are an effective way of reinforcing the message that deception is as equally damaging to your relationship as is acting out.

A relapse in itself does not necessarily mean that the recovery process is not working. If a husband relapses but confesses to his wife within the allotted time period, he is still making forward progress. He is no longer practicing deception. He is walking in the light. He is working the program.

That's not to say that his relapse isn't painful. It is painful because it's sin we are talking about here. Sin *should* feel painful because it's destructive and harmful. This is why your safety plan requires you to put in a call to your support network immediately after a slip. It is the equivalent of forcing you to grab an oxygen mask and take a few good breaths.

When my husband slipped, all the old feelings came flooding back and I fell apart. I was ashamed of where we were again. I thought we were so much farther along than we were. What would people say if they knew I had asked my husband to leave? I remember reaching out to another wife even though I wanted to isolate. But

*I needed that accountability to implement
my safety plan. It was the only way to knock
off all my old codependent habits.* (Mandy)

Making calls in recovery is almost chiropractic. Nothing adjusts an attitude quite like a straight-shooting dose of reality from another addict or another wife. When you are getting out of alignment from the plan, a phone call can jolt you back into alignment.

I remember that when things got heated in the early days of my own recovery, I would take a deep breath, grit my teeth, and say to Mark, "I'm going to make a call and I think *you* need to make a call too."

I've never met "Donnie," the guy on the end of my husband's phone, but I sincerely hope I get to shake his hand one day. God bless Donnie.

Apparently, he would endure my husband's ranting for only so long and then grunt something along the lines of, "You're crazy. *Of course* your wife is angry and hurt. Go back, make her a cup of tea, and shut up." It's probably my weird sense of humor, but I secretly adore the fact that God used a gruff, grumpy recovering sex-addict named Donnie to save my marriage.

Walking in the light is a team sport. Your husband needs to find his tribe and so do you. Being part of a recovery community is the hands-down, absolute best part of all this. If you can't find a support group locally, you may have to create one. But don't panic. I'm going to show you in the next chapter that this is not as hard as it sounds. If this introvert can do it, so can you.

CHAPTER 6

Freedom through Fellowship

"Hi, my name is Rosie, and I am the wife of a man who attends the same group as your husband. It's great that our husbands are getting support, but sometimes I wish that I had support too. I would love to be able to chat with someone else who 'gets it' and wondered if you felt the same. I was thinking of hosting a little informal get-together at my house next month. Is this something you would be interested in attending?"

This was the note that I printed out and gave to Mark to hand out at his weekly support group. I had no idea whether anyone would respond, but I knew I had to try. I could see the difference in my husband after meeting with his "guys" and envied his list of people to call. The only numbers I had were of women I had met at the twelve-step retreat, and they were sex or relationship addicts themselves, not married to addicts.

Three wives responded to my invitation, and we had dinner together at my house. We were all nervous, and I can't remember much of what we spoke about. But just being together was enough. Being able to look into their friendly faces and know that they understood without my having to say a word gave me tremendous comfort. For the first time in months, I didn't feel so alone.

We decided to form our own little group and selected a book on trauma to work through. I lived for those weekly meetings. The rest of the time it felt like I was walking around in a dream—interacting with people but never really there. But for those precious few hours, curled up on my sofa surrounded by the other ladies, my crippling pain would loosen its grip and I could actually breathe. It was the same for all of us. In those early days of shock and bewilderment, the group helped us all stay calm enough to keep going. It was here I learned that God's design was for lasting change to happen in community and here I experienced that community.

Six months later, after a house move and the birth of my first child, I felt much stronger and was ready for the next stage of healing. To this day I still don't know how word spread that I was starting a new group, but on that first Tuesday evening, sixteen ladies showed up at my front door. Sixteen! Sixteen marriages, sixteen wives feeling alone in the battle, sixteen stories that God was redeeming. This was the start of one of the most powerful periods of fellowship I have ever known.

The women came from different churches all over the county. The youngest woman was in her early twenties, the oldest in her seventies. There was much laughter, tears, and cookies, but little small talk. Week after week we heaved up our pain and fears, then fell to our knees and lifted up each other's broken hearts and marriages in prayer. It was messy. It was raw. It was heartbreaking. But the presence of God was palpable. Over the next nine months we slowly turned our eyes away from our husbands and began to look inward. Our husbands' addiction might have gotten us in the door, but we discovered there was much that we needed healing for ourselves now that we were all here together. We steadily worked through material that challenged us to look at our trauma from our past to see how we had developed unhealthy coping mechanisms. We practiced owning our reality and practiced speaking truth to one another in love. It was scary and hard, but weirdly exhilarating too. This is what I had been missing all my life. Real fellowship.

A healthy recovery group is a laboratory for relational intimacy, a safe space for experimenting with how to be authentic, honest, and truth-telling with others before transferring those skills back to your marriage.

Fears of Joining a Women's Recovery Group

"But I've done women's groups before and I just don't like them."

Oh sister, I hear you. One of my most frustrating experiences as a new Christian was attending a weekend women's retreat at a time I was really hurting, yet feeling pressured to walk around saying how "blessed" and grateful I felt. On the last night we gathered around the fire pit and, low and behold, all of sudden everyone started weeping. Out gushed the truth of relationships and families falling apart. It made me want to jump up and down and scream with frustration. What had we been doing for the last forty-eight hours? The missed opportunity for authentic fellowship, not to mention prayer, felt truly tragic. What was the point of having a Savior if no one admitted to needing saving?

I still struggle with women's fellowship that gives the impression that it is possible to get everything right all the time. Just reading about the daily routine of the Proverbs 31 woman makes me want to lie down and take a nap. I get that she's not an actual woman doing everything well in one season of life—she's a mosaic, an ideal, a picture of *all* the seasons of a woman's life put together in one proverb. Still, I'm much more your "woman at the well" sort of gal. As much as I try to put on a smiley façade that I have got it all together, I find it's just too heavy to wear for long. Inevitably, I end up weeping in the bathroom while the children watch Netflix again.

But I'm here to implore you, *please, please, please* don't write off all women's groups because of unsatisfying past experiences.

Trust me—if you're the sort of person who gets frustrated at surface-level fellowship, you're exactly the person who will adore recovery groups.

If you would have told me fifteen years ago that I would be a recovery group junkie, I would have laughed at you. Now I can't wait for the weekly meeting to roll around. Every time I walk in that door, I do a big body sigh. Here I can admit that I don't have it all together, and it doesn't matter because neither does anyone else. I also love the anonymity. Nobody cares who I am. It's positively exhilarating. For a couple of hours, I am not anyone's mom, I am not anyone's wife, I am neither friend nor colleague, I am just here for me. Without fear or filter, I can be myself and tell the truth.

"I'm afraid to open up with people I don't know."

That's not to say going to group in the early days was easy or enjoyable. Walking into my very first twelve-step meeting was terrifying and surreal in equal measure. Maybe I was still in shock, or perhaps I was concussed from hitting my head on the trunk of the car, but I don't remember saying a single word. From talking to other wives, I've found this experience is pretty typical. Most women find they have to push themselves past tremendous fear to walk into the room for the first time.

> I was terrified going to group. What are they going to think? What am I going to say? What if they've never heard this before? Was I safe? Would I know the other

people? Would they recognize me from somewhere? (Shelley)

But here's a promise you can take to the bank. No matter how awful you feel walking into your first group, I guarantee you will not feel the same walking out. Nothing is more powerful than leaving your heavy façade at the door and discovering a whole community of friendly, normal women who have fallen down the same rabbit hole as you.

I was so surprised by how beautiful the women were, and still their husbands acted out. What does that tell you about what I believed about myself? (Shelley)

Turns out I wasn't crazy after all. My red flags WERE red flags. My feelings were okay to have. My expectations were okay to have. My goals and hopes and dreams weren't crazy. (Mandy)

After that first group, I was hungry for more. I wanted more relief, more healing, more encouragement. I couldn't get enough. Anytime there was a meeting, I was there. I needed the validation, the verbal hugs. Everything I was craving I received at those meetings. (Miriam)

What Happens at Group?

There are usually two parts to a meeting: a limited time of check-in, where everyone gets to talk about their week, followed by a time to process the homework they completed the previous week.

During your time of check-in, you get to share whatever you'd like from your week. The most healing parts of the conversation are those in which women are completely honest about what is really going on in their marriage. This is the place to share the things that can't be shared anywhere else. Often just talking about an incident helps, but at other times it might be beneficial to get different perspectives. After living in a household of deception for a long time, it is so helpful to be able to ask, "Am I crazy?" or "Is this really what is going on?"

> *Others saw what I wasn't seeing. They helped me understand what was really going on. They helped me change and do life better. They helped me be free.* (Miriam)

> *Although it wasn't what I always wanted to hear, I would go home and think about what was said. The challenges were hard, but so needed. I wouldn't be where I am today without those women speaking into my life.* (Shelley)

An important part of the group experience is learning how to give feedback in a constructive way. The number one rule to remember is to always ask if the person sharing actually wants to hear feedback. Some people want to use their time to simply vent and be heard, and that is perfectly okay. It's good practice to simply listen to someone expressing pain without jumping in to rescue them.

Making Calls

The growing intimacy between group members is strengthened by regular phone calls. For the first few weeks it is helpful to assign calling partners each week so that you get to know everyone. Find out what time of day works best or set a specific time to call. Also group-text chats can be really useful. This way everyone knows what is happening and can keep up. If someone has an emergency, whoever is free can jump in and help.

Calls are such an essential part of recovery, and yet everyone I know complains about having to make them. Making a call still feels like jumping into a cold pool to me. I always have to brace myself before picking up the phone, but once I'm talking, it's great.

> *Making calls was everyone's nightmare. Being that I'm an extrovert, you'd think making calls would be easy, but it wasn't. I had to be vulnerable and let someone into my life when it wasn't going well. I had never done that before.* (Christy)

Those things that want to stay dark inside of us are hard. When we don't want to reach out, those are the times when we really need to reach out. (Shelley)

When I first got into recovery, I was so out of my skin and emotionally repressed that the thought of calling a stranger and talking about my feelings was truly horrifying. If I hadn't been held accountable to make three calls a week, they would not have happened at all. What got me through those awkward early calls was a laminated "feelings chart" and sticking to a format of expressing three feelings and a need. But after a while I realized I was more scared of receiving calls where I wouldn't be able to "fix it" than of making calls myself. Even though it wasn't my job to fix anyone, I still believed I needed to or was expected to. This was a powerful revelation.

Finding a Group

Although the number of porn ministries is growing, groups for wives are unfortunately still few and far between. If your church is not able to help you locate a nearby group, you might try asking a local CSAT (Certified Sexual Addictions Therapist) for recommendations.

Another option is to think about starting your own group. If you have felt frustrated that there isn't a group locally, I guarantee you are not the only one. Yes, it is intimidating to put yourself out there, but you don't need to place an advertisement in the church bulletin. All you need to do is inform a few key people in leadership and trust God to get the word out.

Running a group is not always easy, but it is a surefire way to strengthen your own recovery. Nothing encourages growth like being in charge. You will share more honestly, complete your homework, and make the required calls. Remember, you are not responsible for anyone's healing. You need to follow the steps, yes, but the healing itself happens by the hand of God! However, the boundaries you set and the expectations you create will set the tone of the group. Here are some guidelines to think about before you begin.

Confidentiality

For the health and safety of the group, it is vital that confidentiality be upheld. What is said in group stays in group. This means that group members may not discuss issues heard with their husbands or other friends. Nothing will derail a group quicker than someone repeating something that was shared in the most sensitive and strictest of confidences.

> When I heard about someone sharing outside the group, I started to hyperventilate. I became flushed and started feeling out of control, like my world was swallowing me up at the same time it was about to explode. It caused a lot of trauma within the group and was hard to recover from. (Mandy)

Have members read and sign a confidentiality agreement as soon as they join. There is only one exception to this rule. If you overhear any disclosure of abuse, report it to your pastoral overseer and the authorities. Doing so is working in cooperation with God's directions for us to love our neighbor, get them out of harm, and obey our governing authorities. When it comes to most things, keep the group's content confidential. But when it comes to abuse, do not keep it confidential. Report it.

Gatekeeping

Deciding who to let into your group is a tricky one. It's tempting to fling wide the gates and accept everyone who says they needs help with their marriage. After all, isn't that what being Christian is all about? However, experience has taught me that groups work best if everyone is there for the same reason with the same goal in mind. Recovery is all about being willing to do hard work and face your own unhealthy ways of coping. You need to be with other women who want to move beyond keeping all the focus on their husbands and make positive changes for themselves. So much of the recovery process understandably focuses on the husband, since his sexual sin led your marriage to this place. However, this women's group should focus on what's going on in *us*, and though that includes details about the husbands and their actions, the goal is to let God work in *our* hearts during this time. If there is a woman who is not committed to letting the Lord work in *her* during this season, she may not be ready for this group.

I found the best way to ensure this is to have a conversation with potential new members beforehand. First, check that their husband actually has a problem with compulsive porn/sex. Second, ask them what they are looking for in a group and see how open they are to looking at their own issues and being gently challenged or sharpened by others. Recovery is for the husband *and* the wife. Any woman in this group needs to be committed to her own healing, recovery, and change.

> *What I loved about group was that everyone wanted to be there. We were a group of women committed to sharing authentically and calling each other on our stuff. We were invested in all of us getting healthy.* (Rebecca)

Rules of Engagement

Having firm rules about how group members communicate with one another during meetings is key to keeping everyone safe. Here are some ideas:

- To avoid certain group members from dominating the discussion, you may find it useful to use a timer to ensure everyone gets an equal opportunity to share.
- During the time of sharing there should be no "cross talk," or interrupting.

- During the time of sharing, everyone should pay attention to the one speaking. No doodling or checking phones.
- Feedback is given following a time of sharing, but only if the person is open to hearing it.
- Comments are most helpful when all stay on topic and lead the sharer to discovering truth.
- Be aware that some people have a tendency to hijack feedback time and swing the conversation back to their own situation. This can be discouraged by emphasizing that the focus needs to stay on the person who has just shared.

Get a Co-facilitator

As facilitator, you need to ensure that everyone sticks to the rules. Inevitably, at some point, you will be required to step in and gently redirect or correct. When this happens, it is useful to have someone to debrief with after the meeting. Having a co-facilitator help you assess how you handled the situation can help you grow in confidence and skill. It's also helpful to split the responsibilities. One of you can focus on practical tasks, like timing the shares, assigning calling partners, and checking up on calls and homework assignments, and the other can focus on facilitating the discussion during the meeting.

Bonus Tip: Come up with a Cover Story Ahead of Time

We live in a small town. More than once I have been at a social function laughing and chatting with a wife I know from recovery and someone asks us how we met. Feeling more than a little awkward about self-disclosing over the chips 'n' dip, I normally panic, turn bright red, and mumble something incoherent. But now my recovery buddies and I have a "cover story" prepared. We simply say something along the lines of that we met at a small group study or through a mutual friend.

I've come to the happy conclusion that the reason this keeps happening is that the obvious affection and easy rapport between myself and the other women in the program lead people to assume that we must have been close friends for decades.

> I love these women. They get it. They under-
> stand where I am, where I have been, what
> I have gone through, because they have
> too. These women don't judge me, or my
> spouse, or our recovery. I can call them and
> I don't get 'Oh I'm soooooooo sorry.' I don't
> get the false sympathetic answer, or some-
> one trying to fix or save me. They listen to
> me. They hear me. I don't have to put on a
> show for these women. (Rebecca)

In terms of what I expect from my friendships, being part of a recovery community has been a game-changer for me. Since experiencing the fullness of authentic fellowship, I have seen most of my relationships change. Recovery has taught me that behind our masks we are all the same. I don't want to go back to wearing a mask, and I don't want to surround myself with people who wear them either. All I want to be is who I was made to be.

Tim Keller sums it up perfectly:

> To be loved but not known is comforting but superficial. To be known and not loved is our greatest fear. But to be fully known and truly loved is a lot like being loved by God. It is what we need more than anything. It liberates us from pretense, humbles us out of our self-righteousness, and fortifies us for any difficulty life can throw at us.[1]

At some point into recovery I realized that the goal was not just about helping my husband get sober from porn and healing my marriage. The truth is, God brought me on this journey *for me,* to heal *me* from codependent ways of thinking, from emotions and behavior that were sabotaging my life, and from harmful patterns I had lived in for a lifetime. God wasn't just stepping on my head to deal with my husband. He was taking me through all this *for me* too.

If you are a wife facing similar circumstances, take heart in that. Amidst all the chaos and hurt and confusion, remember that God is doing something *in you* too. He has not forgotten you. You are not something he needs to half-heartedly deal with in the margins while he expends the majority of his energy on the real issue of your husband. You aren't ancillary, or an afterthought. He sees you, He knows you, and He wants to heal you and change you too in the middle of all this. God is working in all of this *for you* too.

In the next chapter I will show you the transformation that is possible when you are ready to say "Enough" to doing life your way.

CHAPTER 7

♥　　♥　　♥

Your Healing Journey

Do you remember when medicine tasted horrible? When you had to follow it up quickly with a spoonful of jelly or honey? My kids have no idea what I'm talking about. As far as they are concerned, all medicine tastes like bubble gum. In many ways, adding this artificial sweetener is a great improvement. Less tears. Less resistance. But there's also something to be gained from learning that sometimes, what is good for you is often difficult to swallow.

Here's the bitter truth. God also brought you down this path for *you*. To heal *you*. Ending up here was no accident. God intends to use this experience to transform you too, whether you like it or not.

Excuse me? I don't need healing. My husband is the one with the problem.

I get it. I really do. I remember how hurt and mad I was when someone suggested that the implosion of my marriage was somehow my fault. I must have done something wrong if my husband was *that* angry with me. Please, hear me, this is NOT what I am saying. You are in no way responsible for your husband's behaviors or actions. His porn addiction is not your fault. The healing I am talking about is those deep wounds and unresolved griefs that are preventing you from being all that you are meant to be, those ways of coping that served you well as a defenseless child, but are now holding you back as an independent adult.

If I could give you only one piece of advice during this recovery process, it would be this: take your eyes off your husband, and start looking at yourself.

Really Seeing Yourself

The moment you are able to do that, everything will change. Not only in your marriage, but in all your relationships.

Marrying a porn addict and finding myself stranded six thousand miles away from home without a job, friends, or family was not the route to self-awareness and healing I would have chosen, but as crazy as it sounds, it was probably the best thing that ever happened to me. With hindsight I can see God's wisdom in cutting me off from . . . well, everything. Apparently, I needed to be stuck in the middle of nowhere, with an unavailable, blaming husband, before I would face the truth that my romantic relationships were getting progressively worse.

One miserable day, when I was feeling particularly resentful toward Mark for ruining my life, I picked up one of his recovery books to learn more about what was wrong with him. As I read a story of a sex addict whose problems all stemmed from his lack of internal boundaries, a lighthouse-sized light bulb lit up in my head. *This story could have been describing me.* The author's experience was my experience. Could it be possible that I was a bit dysfunctional too? Was I as messed up as my husband? And the truth hit me like a bag of bricks: it was *me* who had blown past red flag after red flag to marry him. True, his sin was not my fault. But the warning signs really were there from the start, and the truth was, my choice of him as a life partner was certainly within my own control. I did everything I could to marry the man, by my own volition. Maybe it was the thought that I could change him—some sort of underlying savior complex—that made me blow right past those obvious red flags. Maybe it was simply the desire to not be alone anymore—a clear indication that God was not enough for me in the moment. Or perhaps it was pride—a belief that once we were married, I'd be more than enough for his sexual appetite, an all-interesting, all-captivating, all-alluring bride. Or maybe it was all those things and more. Regardless of the specifics, the truth was clear: though his sin was real and wrong, and *not my fault,* there really wasn't anyone I could blame for getting myself into this mess in the first place but *me.* I saw sin early on, and I looked the other way. There is much on him, yes, but *that's* on me.

As humbling and painful as my "aha" moment was, it was the critical turning point for me. Acknowledging that I had issues so deep I couldn't even see them was devastating, but by the same token, also strangely empowering. Whether my husband got better or not, I could still work toward becoming healthier and improving *my* life. Being stuck in my victim role, dependent on Mark for my happiness, was making me angry and depressed. But choosing to align myself next to him on a parallel healing track felt purposeful and hopeful. Looking ahead, instead of glaring at each other, we gradually changed from adversaries to allies.

Mark and I were lucky, in the sense that we both "hit bottom" within a few weeks of each other. We'd arrived at our wedding with so much trauma and baggage from past relationships that everything quickly blew up in our faces. This storm had been building for years. I believe God put us together to help in the healing process of the other, but before He could rebuild us, He had to tear us down.

God revealed to me how I had repeatedly self-sabotaged my dream of a happy home and family. As I looked back over my romantic history, He allowed me to see how I had consistently rejected healthy partners who treated me well in favor of less healthy ones who treated me badly. As I observed my crazy brain fantasizing about how the "next" relationship would be the one that would make everything okay, I finally understood how deluded and lost I truly was. I was powerless over making my heart's desire a reality. There would be no loving husband, or children, or Hallmark Christmases for me. Not ever. For two days I lay in bed as though I'd been hit by a truck. I literally couldn't move or stop crying. My idol had been torn down, and me along with it.

Breaking through denial was a brutal, but necessary, stage of my recovery. From that point forward I stopped blaming and shaming my husband and focused entirely on my role in our dysfunctional dance. Yes, he had his issues that he had to own up to. But I couldn't do that work for him. I could only work on *my* issues that *I* needed to own up to. Like a detective, I scoured every book I could find written for women who chose addicts, looking for answers. And there, in the wreckage of my brand-new marriage, I struck gold. I discovered I wasn't uniquely and fatally flawed. I wasn't a masochist. I simply suffered from something called *codependence*. Along with thousands of other people.

Finally, here was a name for my inexplicable self-sabotaging behavior. I felt almost giddy. These books described exactly how I felt and more importantly explained *why* I felt that way. Here were experts telling me it was possible to change. My dream of a happy family wasn't dead in the water after all. There was still hope. Lots and lots of hope.

Am I suggesting that all wives of porn addicts are suffering from codependence? Not at all. But because many wives of porn addicts do identify as codependent, this is the healing model I will be focusing on for the remainder of this chapter. If, however, you can't relate to this model, there are other terms that you might find better applicable to your situation. "Trauma bonding" is another term that often describes how partners of addicts feel—it's the explanation behind why wives will remain in relationship with a batterer. If your relationship is exploitative and traumatic, and yet at the same time the thought of being without your husband is even worse, you may find it helpful to learn more about trauma bonding. I recommend starting with *The Betrayal Bond* by Patrick Carnes. Or maybe you find the term "overcompensating" (parenting versus partnering) more relatable. It matters not how you describe your role in your marriage; what really counts is getting your eyes off your husband and looking instead at the areas where you need healing yourself.

What Is Codependence?

Whenever you rely on an outside source of validation for your self-worth (outside of God), you can be said to be codependent. Everyone does this sometimes, so the reassuring news is that everyone is codependent to some extent. However, when the *only* way you can control how you feel on the inside is by controlling what happens on the outside, you are destined for heartache and trouble. According to Melody Beattie, author of *Codependent No More*, the definition of a codependent is "a person who has let another person's behavior affect him or her, and who is obsessed with controlling that person's behavior." Along with poor self-esteem, common symptoms of codependence include difficulties setting boundaries and problems acknowledging your reality, and expressing it moderately.

Let me translate that for you in terms of my own ongoing struggle with codependence. For example, when my children are expressing negative emotions, I automatically feel responsible. But instead of dealing with my own painful feelings, my codependent instinct is to attempt to control my children. By shutting down their crying or complaints or fears, I won't have to deal with how their negative emotions make me feel. Fortunately, now that I am aware of my underlying codependent tendencies, I consciously stop myself from saying things like, "It's not that bad, for goodness sakes. Stop making that noise!" and instead help them process their emotions. They are now free to work through a negative emotion with me because my happiness, security, sense of worth, and general emotional state is not dictated by their current feelings or behaviors.

Or here's another example: Whenever my husband is just being quiet instead of his usual chit-chatty self, I feel compelled to stop what I am doing and engage with him, not because I want to, but simply to alleviate my overwhelming fear that I have done something wrong. But since working on my codependency, I am able to respond to him with a more discerning spirit, because my actions toward my husband during these times are not simply to make myself feel better or alleviate a lingering sense of guilt. Again, my happiness, security, sense of worth, and general emotional state is not dictated by his current feelings or behaviors. God's Spirit gives me the discernment I need to engage my husband during these moments according to what is actually needed—perhaps he just needs space. Or if he does need to talk, I'm able to get in touch with my own feelings and check if I can be emotionally and mentally present right now. If I decide that I am unable to stop what I am doing without feeling resentful for the interruption, I offer an alternative time when I think I will be able.

Before I entered recovery, it was a totally different story. My struggle with codependence felt like being a helpless puppet, with those closest to me tangled up in the strings. Every time they moved, I reacted. I was hyper-vigilant, stressed, resentful, and deeply lonely. Looking back, I feel heartbroken realizing that the only time I could ever truly relax or feel connected to myself was when I was on my own.

Many times, codependence stems from trauma and early attachment wounds. As one expert says, a "dysfunctional or a less-than-nurturing family system creates children who become codependent adults."[1] Breaking free requires you to examine your childhood and discover how your codependence first took root. Dredging up the past and bringing everything into the light is a painful and exhausting process, but it is the only way to move forward. By getting everything out in the open, you begin to see connections between the painful feelings you experienced as a child and the fact that you will do *anything* to avoid experiencing those same painful feelings today.

Three Dysfunctional "Dances"

When I began the process of uncovering the codependent ways in which I attempt to control painful or confusing situations, I discovered, much to my surprise, that I regularly engaged in not one, but *three* types of dysfunctional dances. I like to think of them as the "Over-Functioning Foxtrot," the "Controlling Tango," and the "Checked-Out Cha-Cha." The names not only help me remember and identify unhealthy ways of coping, but imagining them dressed up in sequins, swirling round a ballroom, somehow makes everything feel less serious and shameful. And thinking about sparkly shoes never hurts.

Strike up the band, get that disco ball spinning, and bring on the dancers. See if any of these dysfunctional coping strategies seem familiar to you.

Over-Functioning Foxtrot

This coping mechanism comes into play when you take on far more than your fair share of responsibilities to prevent anyone from discovering you have a problem in your marriage. Finances, childcare, housework, looking after *your* family, looking after *his* family, you name it—you are the one picking up the slack. Over-functioning and overcompensating may give you and others the illusion of being in control but only for a while. No matter how long or how well you dance, there are no medals. Behind your false smile, you feel crushed, resentful, and exhausted.

Controlling Tango

When you feel so frazzled and out-of-control that you feel like you have to force things back under your control, you're dancing the tango. This dance is always fear-driven and has many faces: tearful scenes, interrogations, verbal abuse, humiliation, threats, and silent punishment. Using emotional brute force to control everyone is exhausting and ineffective and can even backfire. Attention is easily shifted away from the issue at hand and back to *your* over-emotional reaction. Your "paranoia," "nagging," or "craziness" eventually becomes the problem.

Checked-Out Cha-Cha

And now to my favorite go-to, the Checked-Out Cha Cha. The beauty of this dance is that you can do it anywhere, with or without your partner. Feeling sad? Open a bottle of wine. Feeling lonely? Grab a box of donuts and binge-watch a TV show. Feeling resentful? Go shopping. Go on Facebook. Go to a bar. All these examples and more are ways a codependent person checks out of reality and tries to escape. The variations are endless. Avoid reality at all costs, and don't forget to leave your hopes and dreams at the edge of the dance floor.

Introducing a New Dance

For me, the best part of recovery was learning a new dance. An elegant dance. A grown-up dance. The sort of dance that requires a gorgeous frock. My name for it—because, yes, there always has to be a name—is "The Well-Being Waltz." It starts, as all good waltzes do, with a bow and a curtsy. A moment where you literally pause and take a deep breath. A moment where you relinquish responsibility for the other person and take back responsibility for yourself. Here are the signature moves of the Well-Being Waltz:

- You set your own boundaries, guided by Scripture and good counsel.
- You take responsibility for your own hopes, needs, desires, and goals.
- You don't compromise yourself.

- You focus on taking care of yourself (which can look a lot of different ways).
- You get your self-worth from the Lord and not external relationships or circumstances.

To be honest, my waltz is still a bit awkward. Listen closely, and you will hear me repeating the steps under my breath. But I'm finding that the more I practice, the easier it becomes. Healing, I have discovered, is a process. It doesn't happen in an instant.

In the early days of recovery, I prayed so many times for God to take this curse of codependence from me. Yet I remained frustrated and powerless over my compulsion to control everything to avoid my feelings. It wasn't until years later that I realized I needed to get off my knees and start the demanding process of walking it out. Prayer is giving it all to God. Obedience is walking out what He's clearly calling you to do. I was doing the former but not the latter, and it was time to change that.

Codependence never truly goes away, at least not for me so far. It will always be a thorn in my side this side of heaven, it seems. I suppose God loves me too much to let me forget my need for Him. On days when I am emotionally triggered, the urge to control, or over-function, or check out is still there. The voices in my head telling me that I am responsible for everything remain. But by deliberately taking a pause and reminding myself that God is able to do for me what I am not able to do for myself, I find I *am* able to turn the volume down.

Philippians tells us to "Consider others as more important than yourselves" (Phil. 2:3). But the truth is, when I am feeling guilty and fearful, I find it impossible to consider others at all, let alone *above* myself. Is that ever true for you too? It's hard to focus on anything at all when I am on high-alert. Fear keeps me hypervigilant and inwardly focused. Fortunately, the biblical solution is breathtakingly simple and very familiar.

Bring the light to your fight, and let Jesus do the rest. Remember that "the one who conceals his sins will not prosper"— keeping your struggle in the dark will only make it worse! "But whoever confesses and renounces them will find mercy" (Prov. 28:13). All you have to do is drag the struggle in the light.

So what does that look like? How do you walk that out? Well the answer is to first look to the Lord and say along with David, "Finally, I confessed all my sins to you and stopped trying to hide my guilt. I said to myself, 'I will confess my rebellion to the LORD'" (Ps. 32:5 NLT). You simply lay it all bare before the Lord, dragging your issue into the light, asking for His help. Second, you "confess your sins to one another and pray for one another, so that you may be healed. The prayer of a righteous person is very powerful in its effect" (James 5:16). The only action you have to take is telling the truth about yourself, to God first, and then to other people. Once you expose your crippling codependence to the light, let me tell you, *it will lose its power over you.* Confession and repentance were never meant to be scary—remember, Jesus has already paid the penalty for the sin itself. Confession and repentance were meant to be *freeing.* As you bring your issues to the light, God *will* heal you.

Something inside me has changed.

I feel it. My husband feels it. My kids feel it. My codependence is still there, hanging about in the back seat being a nuisance, but it's no longer driving the car. Even when I am emotionally triggered, I am able to consider my family's needs and feelings above myself. I am able to hear my husband express his fears and worries without pulling away or shutting him down. I am able to let my children mess up without spiraling into shame and taking it out on them. I am able to own my uncomfortable feelings and move past them. I don't need the relationships around me to be perfect in order to be okay; I don't need everyone to keep their act together for me to keep mine together; I don't need to control *you* for *me* to be happy. My "okayness" truly comes from the Lord and not my circumstances, and I couldn't say that about myself years ago. My dependency is on God alone, which frees me to interact with others in love instead of in insecurity. This might not seem like a big deal to most people, but to me, it is a miracle.

"But Why Does Healing Have to Be So Painful?"

Great question.

Ten years ago, when my husband's porn addiction picked me up and hurled me down the rabbit hole of recovery, I had no idea I was even in need of healing. If my husband had been just slightly less impossible to live with, I might not have reached out at all. It was pain that forced me onto this path. God allowed it to happen the way it did, not because He didn't love me, but because He did. It's how He works.

Remember those Israelites in ancient Egypt? If life had been at all bearable, would they have ever left? Even after they were miraculously delivered from Pharaoh, it took four decades in the wilderness to strip them of their self-reliance and draw them into right relationship. Forty years to make them utterly dependent on God. Forty years to make them like little children who could enter the Promised Land.

Whether you fight it or embrace it, the truth is that God is using pain to bring you to a place of utter dependence on Him. And it is going to hurt. No one deliberately chooses to be stripped of their self-reliance. Being vulnerable is scary. Who wants to become like a little child who is totally dependent on others? Certainly not me. I fight my sanctification daily. I want answers to my prayers *now*. I want healing for myself and my loved ones *now*.

Yet as I watch my Californian-raised children shrieking and dancing when the rain finally arrives, I am awestruck at their freedom and joy. They don't worry about the future. They never obsess about the past. They trust Mom and Dad will take care of everything they need, and so they simply enjoy the present.

This is the kind of dependence God desires for you. A liberating life-enhancing dependence. A place of freedom and joy, where you can truly be yourself, safe in the knowledge that you have a good Father and that you are a much-beloved child.

> *This journey taught me how to be a whole*
> *person and have value for myself based on*
> *nothing but the fact that I am God's child.*
> *My value is not based on my husband or*
> *my parents or my children or my friends. It*
> *helped me look at my husband in a different*

way also. Now I have grace for him. This was something I was not able to do before. If my husband chooses to do this, that, or the other, I still have value. I am okay with him being imperfect because I am imperfect too. Having experienced the love and grace of God, I am able to extend grace to him. This was so freeing to me. This changed my perspective not only on recovery but also on all my other relationships. There was lots of healing within that. When people told me that dealing with the porn in my marriage would be life changing, I didn't believe them. But it really is. (Miriam)

Being forced to deal with porn in her marriage led Miriam to an abundance of freedom and joy, not only in all her relationships, but also in her faith. Now just think what impact it could have on a church if Miriam's experience was multiplied by fifty wives, or a hundred wives, or a thousand wives? Just imagine what a difference it could make replicated across a nation? What Satan has used for great evil, God could, can, and (I believe) *will* use for great, great good. Just imagine.

Porn is not just destroying ourselves, our relationships, our marriages, and our families, it is crippling our churches too. How can the body of Christ be salt and light to a hurting world, when we are hiding in the shadows because of porn? This is the question we shall be exploring in the next chapter.

CHAPTER 8

♥   ♥   ♥

Bringing Light to the Church's Fight

Some moms are soccer moms. Others are ballet moms. I am an aikido mom. Over the past five years, I have schlepped my son down to the dojo over five hundred times. For those of you who haven't heard of aikido, let me explain. Aikido is a Japanese non-aggressive martial art that teaches you how to defend yourself using the momentum of your opponent's attack to defeat them. It's also seriously cool. A master of aikido appears to have almost superhero powers. Through calm, barely perceptible moves, attackers end up spinning in the air, pinned to the floor and disarmed.

But what I particularly like about aikido, even more than the fact it wears my son out, is that it teaches him a valuable life lesson. Attacks will come. The trick is knowing how to redirect them to your advantage.

There is no way around it. The porn situation in the church is a threat of Goliath proportions. Josh McDowell Ministries spent $300,000 to commission the largest scientific study ever done on pornography in America among pastors, youth pastors, and churched youth and adults. Just listen to what he discovered:

> At least 78.8 percent of all men that attend evangelical churches watch pornography. Probably 80 percent of all evangelical youth pastors also watch pornography, and now, the greatest increase is among women and young ladies. It's killing us. Sixty-four percent of all Christian families have an acute problem with pornography.[1]

yikes!

The Church Needs God's Intervention

But even as the Enemy attempts to use this plague of porn to kill, steal, and destroy, God is redirecting these attacks to our advantage and His glory. The epidemic that is currently devastating the body of Christ, will, I think, be the starting place of revival. It's the ultimate aikido move. Only evil this destructive, and of this magnitude, can bring the church back to a place of repentance and dependence. God is allowing us to pursue our fleshly desires to the point of self-destruction because He is about to do some serious housecleaning. God is allowing our suffering to increase until we are purged of self-reliance and pride that keeps us far from Him. Whatever it takes to get our eyes off ourselves and back onto Him, He will allow. It is the modern-day equivalent of being pressed up against the Red Sea.

By pushing the ancient Israelites right up against the surf— with the full might of the Egyptian army bearing down on them—God brought His people to a new level of dependence. A moment when they had to accept the truth: without God's intervention, they were done for.

In terms of where porn is taking the church, without God's intervention, we too are goners.

Just as there comes a point in every porn-invaded marriage when a wife is forced to deal with it, the same thing is happening in the marriage between Christ and His wife, the church. The pressure is building. Rapidly. Because of the mounting evidence linking porn use to a breakdown in family values, and a whole host of other negative public health issues, ignoring the porn issue in our country (and world!) is becoming increasingly problematic. Every day we remain silent is another day our families fall apart, another day we walk right past injustice and suffering on a monumental scale:

- Women and men brutalized and discarded by the porn industry
- Women, men, and children being trafficked and filmed
- Women and men being violently assaulted
- Children being sexualized and abused
- Children acting out what they have seen with other children

- Young men demanding that young women perform the acts they've seen on screen, even when it causes bodily harm
- Young men crippled by erectile dysfunction
- Husbands unable to be aroused by their actual wife
- Men, women, and children hopelessly addicted

When will we, as the body of Christ, be ready to acknowledge that the battle against porn is here, it's bloody, and it's taking place right inside our sanctuary walls? Despite 92 percent of senior pastors saying porn is a "much bigger" problem for the church now compared to twenty years ago,[2] only 7 percent of them report that their church has a ministry program for those struggling with porn.[3]

For far too long we have remained awkwardly on the sidelines, while our families and brains literally disintegrate, euphemizing porn as everyman's "struggle" and laughing about its references that are well woven in our favorite TV shows. While important not to shame men and women who are "struggling," shying away from talking directly about porn has had the unwanted effect of despiritualizing and normalizing it.

There is nothing normal about pornography.

Porn use must never be casually lumped in with the other sins of the flesh like overeating, or overworking, though the consequences of those sins are very real and damaging. With porn, we have to remember that every click contributes to the demand for further exploitation and abuse. For people who grew up before Internet porn, it is hard to comprehend what horrors are now available with a few taps on a screen. Porn is not naked women gazing seductively at a camera, though that alone would not be acceptable. Porn is way beyond watching consenting adults having sex, though again, that would be destructive as well. Pornography, as it is today, is an unimaginable world of brutality and cruelty, based on dominating and dehumanizing women and children.

In an analysis of the fifty most popular porn scenes, 85 percent of scenes contained physical violence, and 49 percent contained verbal aggression.[4] In "real life" these acts of aggression would be rightly called abusive. But how do the women in porn react? With shock and distress? With outrage? Nope, think again. Ninety-five percent of the time, women in porn respond to acts of aggression neutrally or with expressions of pleasure. You really need to get this. *Porn teaches that women are aroused by verbal and physical abuse.* Women like being called derogatory names, they enjoy being slapped, gagged, having their hair pulled and much worse. Porn teaches that rape victims enjoy being raped.[5]

Where Porn Is Taking Us

The two biggest trends on the demand side in the porn industry today are for younger victims and more violent sexual behavior. Put this together with porn being addictive and progressive in nature, and what you have is an increasing demand for child victims. Two million children are trafficked around the world annually, 300,000 of those in the United States—*children whose documented sexual abuse is then sold as child porn.* Seventy percent of underage human trafficking victims report that they were used to create pornographic videos while they were enslaved.

And just when you think things can't possibly get any worse, child sexualization has been destigmatized to such an extent that there is now a cultural movement called MAP (Minor-Attracted-People) who are asking for acceptance for their sexual preferences. They have even appropriated their own version of a Pride flag. As long as the porn industry can capitalize off pedophilia, they will keep the "barely legal" videos coming. I'll say it again: porn is not neutral or funny. It's not every person's "struggle." It's every person's *poison*, and we need to start acting as if that's true, and vomit it out of our churches.

Salt and Light

Christians are called to be salt and light in the world. We are meant to shine a light into the dark corners of society and preserve moral decency. We should be the ones protesting the most effectively about the commercial sexual exploitation of women and children. We ought to be the ones making sure everyone sees the link between porn and increasing sexual violence. We should be outraged when we see eroticized, misogynistic rage marketed as educational, entertaining, and empowering.

We should be, but we're not.

No, we're hiding in the shadows, feeling condemned and ashamed because we've fallen short, or rather our husbands have fallen short; and we're believing the lie that we're somehow responsible. We don't want to talk about it. We don't even want to think about it. It's too painful. We are paralyzed. It's hard to raise our hands in praise on a Sunday morning, knowing full well what is really going on behind our closed doors. There's no way we can stand up and protest against porn when we are part of the problem.

When statistics tell us that almost as many Christians as non-Christians are regularly looking at porn, it makes good business sense for the church to keep a low profile on this issue. At least until it can clean up its act. In these seeker-sensitive times, the last thing Christians need to do is appear hypocritical. A church full of porn addicts? That's hardly a good Christian witness, is it?

Or, is it?

Struggling with porn does not make us bad Christians; it makes us humans in desperate need of a Savior. The truth is, we live in a fallen world, and in our flesh we still war against all that is good and holy. "For all have sinned and fall short of the glory of God" (Rom. 3:23). Becoming Christian does not improve our flesh. Becoming Christian does not guarantee we will never struggle with porn again. Even the apostle Paul, the greatest evangelist who ever lived, refers to himself as the "chief" of sinners (1 Tim. 1:15 NKJV). Even though the Holy Spirit now dwells in us—giving us the desire to do good—sin still resides in us. This is the tension that causes so much pain. We want to do what is right, and yet we don't. We want to stop looking at porn, and yet we don't. Listen to how Paul describes his internal wrestling with the problem of sin in him in Romans 7:14–25 (NIV):

We know that the law is spiritual; but I am
unspiritual, sold as a slave to sin. I do not
understand what I do. For what I want to do
I do not do, but what I hate I do. And if I do
what I do not want to do, I agree that the law
is good. As it is, it is no longer I myself who do
it, but it is sin living in me. For I know that
good itself does not dwell in me, that is, in my
sinful nature. For I have the desire to do what
is good, but I cannot carry it out. For I do not
do the good I want to do, but the evil I do not
want to do—this I keep on doing. Now if I do
what I do not want to do, it is no longer I who
do it, but it is sin living in me that does it. So
I find this law at work: Although I want to do
good, evil is right there with me. For in my
inner being I delight in God's law; but I see
another law at work in me, waging war against
the law of my mind and making me a prisoner
of the law of sin at work within me. What a
wretched man I am! Who will rescue me from
this body that is subject to death? Thanks be to
God, who delivers me through Jesus Christ our
Lord! So then, I myself in my mind am a slave
to God's law, but in my sinful nature a slave to
the law of sin.

I find it incredibly freeing to remember that we are no better or no worse than people two thousand years ago. Lust, rage,

pride are the same today as they were when Jesus walked the earth. If the Romans had invented the Internet, you can be sure that they would be streaming live from the Colosseum. The only difference between sexual immorality in biblical times and today is accessibility. Technological advances are just helping us indulge our inherent natures more efficiently, frequently, and creatively. The current statistics, although gut-wrenching and heartbreaking, are not surprising.

It is not porn use that prevents Christians from being salt and light, it is our pride and self-reliance. We would rather isolate and self-medicate than admit to one another that we might not have everything together. Our leaning toward lust is only matched by our love affair with reputation management.

Reputation Management

When the level of dirt in my house gets past the point of no return, making it clear that it might be time to hire a professional cleaner, I am always amazed at how long I spend tidying up before they arrive. Sure, part of me doesn't want to pay good money for someone to wash my dishes and pick up toys, but there's also a part of me that doesn't want my cleaner to think that I'm the sort of person who "needs" a cleaner. Do you see how crazy that is? I want the person I am paying to clean my house to think I am much better at keeping my house clean than I really am. Even though they are the one who will discover how disgusting my shower is, I still try and fool them.

We do exactly the same thing with our sin. All the time.

The last thing we want to do is confess any weaknesses or failures. We will do anything to avoid admitting that we are still very much the type of sinner that Jesus came to save. We don't mind being seen as the person who *used* to have a problem, but now . . . well, now we are completely healed and living a perfect life, thank you very much. No matter how grateful we are having a Savior to forgive us for our past sins, we still resist—with all our might—the fact that we still very much need one.

Being a sinner who truly needs Jesus is not an enviable experience. Although I adore reading the stories in the Bible where Jesus redeemed the bleeding woman (Mark 5:25–34), the woman caught in adultery (John 8:1–11), the woman at the well (John 4:4–26), and the woman who wept on Jesus' feet (Luke 7:36–50; John 12:1–8), I would never want to trade places with them. I can only imagine what each of them went through to get to the point of meeting Jesus. They had nothing to offer Him but their pain, desperation, and sin.

Needing a Savior is excruciating. It's humiliating. That's where the word *humility* comes from. It's painful and lowly and gut-wrenching.

It was painful for people in the Bible, and it's just as painful for us today.

When I talk about my own journey of becoming a Christian, I can honestly say that it was the pain of my sinful lifestyle that propelled me into the pews. God blessed me by letting me experience in a very real way that I had nothing to offer Jesus but my brokenness. There was no way I could pretend to be anything other than exactly the sort of person Jesus came to save. "It is not those who are healthy who need a doctor, but those who are sick. I have not come to call the righteous, but sinners to repentance" (Luke 5:31–32).

So why do I sometimes catch myself envying other Christians when I hear their testimonies of coming to faith at age six, marrying their childhood sweetheart, and doing "respectable" ministry helping orphans in some far-flung country? It's the same reason part of me wishes someone else had their name on this book, and that my children had a mom that wrote children's fiction, not books about dealing with porn. *What a wretched ungrateful woman I am!*

Despite the incomprehensible gift of grace I have been given, I would still prefer to downplay exactly why I need it. Basing my sense of self-worth on what Jesus did for me, rather than from what I do, is a constant struggle. Being transparent and vulnerable in a judgmental world is an act of faith. My spirit desperately wants to please God by being faithful, but my flesh craves the approval of other people.

Thankfully, God is not shocked by weakness when it comes to reputation management. He created me. He is well aware that if I could find a way to pull myself together and stop being a willful, easily-spooked, silly sheep, I would even ditch my Shepherd.

Jesus knows all this and loves me anyway.

The only way I can begin to relate to this level of insane love is by thinking about my own children. When my boys steal my ENTIRE box of chocolates, scream that they hate me, and throw epic tantrums, I do not love them less. That's not to say I like them very much at the time, and that I won't discipline them, but I still would lay down my life for them in an instant.

This is how God feels about us.

This is what He has already done for us.

He knows we are obsessed with managing our reputations, but He meets us right in the middle of that ridiculousness and helps us move past it.

Our Living Hope

God has already provided us with a solution. He has made a way out. By sending His Son Jesus to the cross to die, He has already paid the price for *all* our sin, including all the pride, and all the porn in the world. He paid the price so that there is now "no condemnation for those in Christ Jesus" (Rom. 8:1). Through His blood we have been acquitted. Shame no longer holds us captive. Because of what He did, we can walk boldly in the light whatever our sins, confident in the knowledge that we are miraculously, and unfathomably, clothed in His righteousness. We have nothing to fear about telling the truth. "Who shall bring a charge against God's elect? It is God who justifies. Who is he who condemns?" (Rom. 8:33–34 NKJV).

We say we are people who love Jesus. We say we have faith. But are we acting like we have faith when it comes to porn? By hiding in the shadows, refusing to talk about it, we are giving the message that there are particular "sins" that can separate Christians from the love of God. *Real Christians don't struggle with porn; you really ought to keep that issue hidden.*

If we want to turn this battle around, we have to relentlessly preach that *nothing* can separate you from the love of God, not even your husband's porn use (or your porn use, if you're the one fighting the desire to run to it). Jesus' blood is enough to cover continual porn watching from this day forth until the time you die. That is not to say you should! Paul would say it this way: "Should we continue in sin so that grace may multiply? Absolutely not! How can we who died to sin still live in it?" (Rom. 6:1–2).

Only a message of pure unadulterated grace will strengthen our faith enough to obey God. We have to know that we are safe to come out of the shadow before we will take a step toward the light.

It doesn't make sense to our human flesh to come forward and admit our most shameful secrets and expose our weakness. But when we obey God, and walk in the light, we are acting like people of faith. Remember, "without faith is it impossible to please God" (Heb. 11:6). We are saying "Yes, I believe—I have faith that I'm safe to come out of the shadow because there is no penalty waiting for me from God. I may have to face my consequences, but I have faith that real change is available to me. I believe God is *that* good, and that His gospel covered *that* much and more."

Captivity to porn is forcing us to act like people of faith who trust and obey their God. What I mean here is that the church's porn use is forcing us to publicly show the world that Christians are just as tempted by porn as they are! But the big difference in the two is that we have a great hope in Christ. Of course, we *want* to fix our porn problem quietly in a dark corner, but overcoming porn in the light, through the power of Christ, gives all the glory to God.

> "You are the light of the world. A city situated on a hill cannot be hidden. No one lights a lamp and puts in under a basket, but rather on a lampstand, and it give light for all who are in the house. In the same way, let your light shine before others, so that they may see your good works and give glory to your Father in heaven." (Matt. 5:14–16)

This is how the church will become like a city on a hill, shining brightly for all to see. Not because it doesn't have a porn problem, but because it boldly admits that it does—all the while pointing to the only One who can break its stronghold. When we come out into the light and own our sin before the watching world, we are showing them that it's safe to come out of hiding when it comes to God. We can repent, because we actually believe the payment is covered and healing is in our future. We are saying to the world that God is worth more to us than our reputation, and we have faith that He can actually change us!

Dealing with That Little Voice

Theologian Martin Luther is often quoted as saying, "When the Devil accuses you, plead guilty, and point to Jesus." Actually, this is what he said (but's it not quite as catchy):

When the devil throws our sins up to us and declares we deserve death and hell, we ought to speak thus: "I admit that I deserve death and hell. What of it? Does this mean that I shall be sentenced to eternal damnation? By no means. For I know One who suffered and made a satisfaction on my behalf. His name is Jesus Christ, the Son of God. Where he is, there I shall be also."[6]

So, remember, when that little voice whispers in your ear that you aren't strong enough or brave enough to go through this process, plead guilty and point to Jesus. Agree with the assessment. Yes, you are broken and terrified. And it's absolutely true that in your own strength, you would undoubtedly fail. But remember: you are not doing this in your strength. Your hope is in the Lord. Your "help comes from the LORD" (Ps. 121:2). The Lord God Almighty is on your side, and He will be victorious through you. For "with God all things are possible" (Matt. 19:26).

And the next time you start to worry that people will assume there's something wrong with you if they find out that your husband struggles with porn, take a deep breath and say to yourself, "Ha! If they only knew the half of it!" The truth is, there's probably *a lot* more wrong with both you and your husband than anyone knows! And it's okay to say that—it's the truth about every single human being on the planet. We're all *far* worse than what we project in the world. Instead of playing perfect, plead totally guilty. Yes, there are hundreds of things

wrong with you, but you are covered by the blood of Jesus and
have already been granted right standing with God.

Jesus never argued with the devil. He just hit him with
Scripture. Here's a wonderful passage to have up your sleeve.
The next time Satan tries to mess with you, sock him between
the eyes with this.

> What, then, shall we say in response to these
> things? If God is for us, who can be against us?
> He who did not spare his own Son, but gave
> him up for us all—how will he not also, along
> with him, graciously give us all things? Who
> will bring any charge against those whom God
> has chosen? It is God who justifies. Who then
> is the one who condemns? No one. Christ Jesus
> who died—more than that, who was raised to
> life—is at the right hand of God and is also
> interceding for us. Who shall separate us from
> the love of Christ? Shall trouble or hardship or
> persecution or famine or nakedness or danger or
> sword? As it is written:
>
> > "For your sake we face death all day long;
> > we are considered as sheep to be
> > slaughtered."
>
> No, in all these things we are more than con-
> querors through him who loved us. For I am
> convinced that neither death nor life, neither
> angels nor demons, neither the present nor

the future, nor any powers, neither height nor
depth, nor anything else in all creation, will be
able to separate us from the love of God that is
in Christ Jesus our Lord. (Rom. 8:31–39 NIV)

How's that for a nifty aikido move? Instead of trying to
block out accusations by denying them, better to simply agree to
the truth of your human condition, and use Scripture to bring
Jesus into the fight. Agree with the accusation—you really *are*
that messed up. And then agree with God—you really *are* that
forgiven and loved.

Becoming a City on a Hill

My husband and I have had the privilege of being invited
into many people's lives at a time when it seems like there's no
hope for their marriage. A time where the damage caused by the
betrayal of porn or sex addiction seems insurmountable. When
trust is down to a feeble flicker. Yet, time after time, as husbands
and wives commit to rigorous honesty, we have seen marriages
not only restored but also radically transformed. These couples
courageously choose to walk in the light and are profoundly
changed.

> Our marriage did a complete one-eighty. All
> the energy that my husband was using to
> pursue his addiction, is now turned toward
> me. Now he is loving me in a manner that I
> didn't even know was possible. He also has

*boundless energy for our family, for God,
and for other people. It has been amazing
to watch.* (Shelley)

No pastor wants to admit the truth that a significant proportion of their congregation is struggling with porn, any more than a wife wants to admit that her own husband is struggling, but dragging the fight into the Light, where "everything exposed by the light is made visible" (Eph. 5:13) is the *only* way to turn it around.

Lives are transformed when people physically experience the grace and love of God through brutally honest fellowship. It's time to stop performing, cease the reputation management— whether that's as individuals, as a marriage, or as a church—and get real. The stakes are now too high for half-hearted measures. All of us need to drop our masks, reveal that we are all messed up in some way or another, and help dismantle the barriers of shame that prevent people coming forward for help. Confessing our sins, one to another, needs to become an everyday act of all faithful Christians, and not something special that only happens in "recovery groups."

Praise God for using this epidemic of porn to push the church up against the Red Sea, where we will have no choice but to start living "as children of light" (Eph. 5:8). Just imagine what it would look like if everyone at your church, including staff, was open and unashamed about their need for a great and mighty Savior? Can you hear how loud and passionate the worship is? Can you see the people praying on their knees? Can you see them holding one another? Can you feel the love between them?

Can you hear the laughter, see the tears? Look at all the people pouring through the doors.

If all Christians were actually living according to the Bible, porn addiction wouldn't even exist in the church. Addiction is thriving because our performance-based façade keeps us isolated and secretive, making the ground extra fertile. If a person did look at porn, they'd confess it straight away, so that the desire wouldn't be able to take root and turn into a habit. For "everything exposed by the light becomes visible—and everything that is illuminated becomes a light" (Eph. 5:13 NIV).

As the church in the world, we don't need more human-centered effort. We don't need better reputations. What we need is to boldly step into the light, dragging all our junk along with us even if it requires our humiliation, let Jesus and His gospel do the work of healing, and give God all the glory. Honesty. Brokenness over sin. Confession. Repentance. Redemption. Community. Healing. Worship. Wouldn't that be a sight for the world to behold?

CHAPTER 9

♥ ♥ ♥

Women Who Struggle with Porn

As much as things have improved in our country in terms of equal opportunities for women, there's an awful long way to go in terms of double standards. Women who struggle sexually are still viewed in a whole different category than men. Boys who look at porn are dismissed as, "boys just being boys." But girls who watch porn . . . hang on a minute, girls watch porn?

> *I told my pastor's wife that I had a problem with pornography, and she told me I was confused. Romance novels were not pornography. I felt so bad, I lied. How could I say I was doing hard-core porn for hours every day after that?* (Shawnee, age 24)

But to be fair to that well-meaning pastor's wife, compulsive porn never used to be an issue for females the way it was for males. However, with the onset of the Internet era, everything changed. Today, one out of every four porn users is female (26%).[1] By the time this book hits the shelves the actual percentage will be even higher. That's how quickly things are progressing.

The Numbers Are Going up for Women Viewing Porn

With the male market saturated, and children being effectively targeted, it's women who are the final frontier for the marketers of the porn industry. It's women who are being deliberately sold the lie that porn is empowering and that it will enhance their relationships.

Tragically, it's working.

Here are the numbers of women who view pornography (at least monthly) broken down by age. The generation gap between older and younger women is telling.

> *Thirty-five percent of women between the ages of 18 and 30.*
>
> *Twelve percent of women between the ages of 31 and 49.*
>
> *Ten percent of women between the ages of 50 and 68.*

To get an idea of what is happening in the church, half those figures.[2] Give it ten years, and this will become one of the biggest issues among Christian women. Mark my words. Youth pastors report that one in five high school girls (23%), and one in ten (10%) middle school girls, have approached them for help with pornography.[3] The only ones who are not shocked by these statistics are the kids themselves.

Porn stealthily snakes its way under a girl's defenses, until addiction has her in a stranglehold. For girls who do not have much of a sexual history and are not sexually active, this process is even more dramatic. Research has proven that the less sexually "experienced" you are, the more attention bias you give to sexually stimulating material.[4] In other words, the more innocent you are, the more potent you will find porn. Mothers of daughters be aware: porn is kryptonite for virgins. I hate to put it that way, but it's true.

> I was a good kid. I came from a solid Christian home with married parents, an older sister, and a dog. I got straight A's in school, danced in a ballet company, took piano lessons, and competed with a swim team. I had friends. I went to church every Sunday, attended Pioneer Girls, and sang in the choir. No one, especially not my parents, ever had reason to suspect I was hiding a secret.
>
> After all, I was a good kid.
>
> But I was also a curious kid, and at times, a lonely one. An innocent Google search of "how to kiss" can get you far in a matter of

clicks at an unmonitored monitor. By the age of ten, I was a full-blown pornography addict, spending hours a day shooting up X-rated material from the safety of my closed bedroom.

I was still a good kid. But I was lost.

Terrified of disappointing the people I loved most. Terrified of making my parents feel like failures at the job they gave their hearts to. Terrified of the wrath of a God waiting to throw me into hell.

And so I was silent.

For seven years of my childhood, I fought my battle alone, trapped inside a computer screen, listening to the same soundtrack loop in my head: "You are disgusting. You are vile. Keep your head down and your mouth shut or you'll expose how sick and broken you really are. No one else struggles like you do; you are the only one, and if you open up, you will destroy the people who love you. Everyone will reject you. God will reject you."

No one actually told me these things. Certainly, the church didn't. But no one told me the opposite, either. I was never told that girls and children struggle with pornography too. Everyone was silent. And *the Enemy filled the silence with lies.* (Lily, age 20)

Dismantling the Myths of Women and Sexual Sin

Girls, like Lily, desperately need someone to break the lies and the silence for them. We have to start discussing this taboo topic openly and regularly. The church is making great strides in breaking the shame surrounding porn addiction for men and boys, but now we must do the same for women and girls.

The first step is to dismantle the myth that women are not capable of sinning sexually in the same ways as men. They are made as much in the image of God, and they are likewise cursed as much under the Fall too. The call to give up sexual sin is an equal-opportunity command for both genders to obey.

Jesus did not look at the woman caught in adultery and tell the crowd, "This woman did not really want to have sex with a man who wasn't her husband; she was just lonely and wanted company." No, He looked her straight in the eye, confronted her sin, and forgave her. He did not cheapen His grace by denying the severity of her sin. He treated her as an equal image-bearer, meaning He spoke directly to her about her sin and did not go through someone else. He saw her as able to face the reality and the consequences of her sin, and treated her as a grown-up, right where she was, in the muck and the mire of her situation. He treated her as valuable and worthy simply by shooting her straight. As the only one with the "legal right" to punish her, He chose to take her punishment, and give her His righteousness. His grace, not her behavior, was the true scandal.

Let's stop pretending that women aren't capable of being lured into sexual sin just as easily as men. And while we are myth-busting, let's also crush the ridiculous notion that women only watch porn because they secretly want to enact it. The reality is that when women actually experience the sexual acts seen in porn videos, they largely react with shock and disgust, not surprise and delight.[5] And even when a woman, with a porn-altered arousal template, does ask her partner to act out what she has been watching, this behavior inevitably causes problems in the relationship. Instead of feeling empowered and fulfilled, the woman eventually ends up feeling disgusted and frustrated with herself (more on this later).

Here's the bottom line: the poison of porn does not discriminate. Because of compulsive porn use, increasing numbers of both men *and* women are being distanced from God, having their moral compasses re-calibrated, their relationships wrecked, and their brains physiologically rewired to compulsively seek out increasingly destructive and degrading material.

Women's Brains on Porn

According to the statistics, women are now actually viewing more violent, and more extreme, genres of porn than men.[6] Yes, that's right. More rough or harmful sex. More gang scenes. The reason I am telling you this is not to shock you, but to disabuse you of the notion that women, because of their compassionate nature, are somehow more able to protect themselves from getting pulled into viewing really disturbing material. Despite what you might have heard about women not being visually aroused, as it turns out, our brains are just as susceptible to porn as men's.

When it comes to sexual stimuli, neuroscience has proven that porn has far more sway over women's brains than we may have been led to believe. Thomas James, a neuroscientist at Indiana University, who works with researchers at the Kinsey Institute for Research in Sex, Gender, and Reproduction, says, "When we put people in the functional magnetic resonance imaging (fMRI) scanner and show them sexual stimuli, the response in the brain is two to three times stronger than any other kind of image or stimulus I've ever used."[7]

Our brains, it would seem, are fine-tuned for porn—and this tell-tale brain activation response happens in both men and women. When viewing porn, both male and female brains light up like Christmas trees. And although women may have a reputation for demanding lengthy foreplay, they actually become sexually aroused just as quickly as men. According to a study that used thermal imaging to measure increased blood flow to genital regions both sexes reach peak arousal within 10 minutes of watching porn—men 665 seconds; women 743 seconds.[8]

Let's be clear, if women wanted romance, they would be firing up Netflix not porn sites. Whether it comes to "soft" forms of porn or the typical Internet pornography that's out there, women are using it in the same way and for exactly the same reasons as men. Remember, it is the urge to keep the powerful hits of dopamine coming, not the content itself, that compels users to keep on clicking.

Living a Double Life Addicted to Porn

It is estimated that one in five women are addicted to porn.[9] And increasingly, it is being recognized that women may actually have a higher risk of addiction. Let me repeat that—women may have a *higher* risk of addiction. This is because women don't need as long a recovery period after climaxing as men and are able to go on "porn binges." Because of the preconceived notion that women don't watch porn, let alone get addicted to it, women who compulsively use it assume that there must be something seriously wrong with them. Believing that they are the only ones, they live in constant fear of being found out.

> *At school, I'm known as the "Christian girl" who doesn't do anything bad. I've just been asked to be a leader at my youth group, and everyone thinks highly of me. I want to ask for help, but I'm too scared. I can't tell my parents; they would be so disappointed.*
>
> *After a whole week of not doing anything, I gave in again, today. What does it matter anyway? I'm supposed to share my testimony at church on Sunday. Just thinking about it makes me feel sick. How can I talk about loving Jesus knowing what I am. I do want to change. I know I should tell*

someone, but if I do, no one will ever look at me the same again. My life will be ruined forever." (Sarah, age 17)

As we have already learned in chapter 2, when porn users engage in more compulsive behavior, their neuropathways become desensitized to the types of pornographic images they are used to seeing, and they are driven to seek more extreme material to achieve the same level of arousal. For female addicts, this means being sucked into a world of misogynistic depravity that eats their soul from the inside-out.

> *The porn I would watch had a common theme. Most were violent, all were degrading. The more people the better. I found disturbing things arousing. Unhealthy things became really attractive to me. Just thinking about them would intoxicate me. Watching porn wasn't shameful enough for me. I needed darkness. To be disgusted. To be traumatized.* (Jude, age 34)

Women who struggle with porn talk of living a double life riddled with fear, uncertainty, and hopelessness. In the cold light of day, they feel deeply ashamed at the material they are compelled to seek out in the heat of a porn binge. It's disturbing and confusing to realize that when they are turned on, the pain and suffering of the women on film is not enough to make them switch it off. However, a recent study offers an alternative explanation for this apparent lack of feeling during arousal.

Women Emotionally Shut Down during Porn

Researchers in the Netherlands have discovered, with the help of a PET scanner, that part of women's brains shut down while watching pornographic videos. "At the moment of orgasm, women do not have any emotional feelings," says Gert Holstege of the University of Groningen.[10] "It was unbelievable, very pronounced. You see extreme deactivation of large portions of the brain, especially the fear centers, the brain that controls emotions." Basically, the brain can either be anxious or aroused (or neither), but not both. No matter how compassionate a person you are, or are how strident your personal convictions are, if you are aroused enough while watching pornography, your feelings (which would usually signal that what you are engaging is wrong) will be over ridden. Watching pornographic material shuts down your good and God-given emotional center.

It's also important to mention that because of the way that women interact with porn, it can also warp ideas about sex. Unlike men, who are primarily aroused by objectification, women project themselves right into the pornographic action.[11] Arousal for a woman is dependent upon her ability to imagine herself as the object of desire. This happens with romance novels and movies, and this happens with porn. This is the way we are wired. And for some women, constant exposure to hardcore porn can actually rewire their arousal template, literally brainwashing them into thinking this is what they *want*.[12] And when a woman can only become aroused when she is being degraded and abused, she is imprisoned in a whole new level of evil. This self-destructive enslavement is devastating for her soul and her psyche, and is a far cry from the promised "female empowerment" pedaled by the pro-porn propaganda machine. No woman seeks to be degraded, hurt, and humiliated from a place of wholeness and healthy self-esteem.

> *Sex with my husband was upsetting for both of us. He didn't feel comfortable doing the things that I wanted him to do, things that I needed him to do. It upset him that I wanted to be treated in that way, and I hated the fact that I needed to get the old tapes going in my head in order to feel aroused. My husband said it feels like I am never really there, and he is right.* (Sasha, age 28)

The cruel irony is that while porn addiction causes women to be sexually charged, it also impairs sexual responsiveness. In forums all across the Internet, women are coming forward with their own version of "porn impotence": a loss of sensation and arousal during real-life sex with their spouses. What the articles telling women to spice up their relationships with porn always fail to mention is that the spice they are recommending is arsenic.

What to Do If You Are Struggling

If you are a Harry Potter fan, you will be familiar with the underground plant called Devil's Snare. This deadly vine constricts around any living thing that falls into it. Only exposure to a bright light will make the plant recoil. But for those trapped in the dark being slowly strangled, the key to escaping is to stop fighting and relax. Struggling only makes the problem worse.

As counterintuitive as it seems, the only way to escape porn is to surrender. I don't mean surrendering as in give in and watch porn whenever you feel the need. No, surrendering as in give up the notion that you can handle the problem alone. You have to get this problem into the light and invite others in to help you. Struggling alone in the dark will only make the problem worse.

However, I understand why the shadows are preferable. It's hard to share your struggles when you don't know how people will react. Will you be treated differently? How do you admit to having a problem that doesn't apparently exist?

The key is finding the right person to confide in. Pray about it, and ask God to show you who the right person is. Ideally this would be a counselor or therapist trained in sex/porn addiction, or a woman who "gets it" through personal experience. But where that isn't possible, find someone you trust. Someone who you know is open and transparent about their own struggles— whatever they may be. The last thing you need is to be in a one down position. Feeling like the identified patient makes opening up excruciating. You need real fellowship with someone who will take your struggle seriously and will help you get the support you need without making you feel judged.

The journey out of addiction is exactly the same for women as it is for men. Women require the same degree of expertise from their counselor, the same loving firm boundaries from their partner, and the same healing community of fellow addicts.

Being committed to radical honesty with God, with yourself, and with others will produce a radical transformation. Total freedom is possible.

When seeking help, choose counselors or therapists who are qualified to treat sexual addiction. See my resources page on my website for up-to-date links to training organizations and their national databases. On this page, I also list a number of excellent online ministries that deal specifically with female porn addiction. Founded by recovering addicts, they provide a proven path out of addiction and an instant community that "gets it." However, in addition to utilizing online resources and support groups, I'm going to stress again how vital it is to tell someone in person. As Jessica Harris, author, public speaker, and recovering porn addict, warns, "Anonymity is one of the things that can draw women to pornography and it's one of the things that can keep them there."

Speaking as one who has walked the walk, and successfully battled free from her own addiction, Jessica also has great advice for pastors, women's ministry leaders, youth pastors, and teachers. "If a girl or woman comes to you confessing a struggle with pornography, it is because you are her last hope. The only reason she is talking to you is because her addiction scares her more than the idea of people finding out. Make no mistake. It is a desperate cry for help. And if you walk away, she may never confess again."[13]

We are all responsible for a church culture where women are too ashamed and afraid to come forward for help. By the same token, we all have the potential to change it. The first step is to

acknowledge that the way we talk about women who use porn—
or, in most cases, don't talk about them—has a real impact on
those women struggling.

As followers of Christ, we ought to be leading the way in
terms of breaking the shame. Jesus wouldn't leave women suffering silently in the pews. Just look at His ministry. Have you ever
noticed that the encounters between Jesus and those ostracized,
condemned, and persecuted for sexual sin were always women?
Isn't that fascinating? It was no accident that these particular stories were immortalized in sacred history. Through His actions,
Jesus not only redeemed and transformed the lives of individual
women, but He also challenged everyone else's preconceived
ideas and prejudices about women in general.

Let's do a quick recap. In the case of the woman caught in
the act of adultery (John 7:53–8:11), Jesus rejected the double
standard for women and men, and turned the judgment upon
the male accusers. On another occasion, in John 4:1–42, Jesus
defies cultural and religious conventions by reaching out to
a Samaritan women at the well. Not only was she a despised
Samaritan and a woman, but she also had been married five
times. Yet Jesus did not shun her. He not only welcomed her,
but also revealed Himself to her as the Messiah she longed to
know. In astonishment and gratitude, she spread the good news
of Christ, every bit a newly devoted disciple and evangelist.

Then in Luke 7:36–50, Jesus permits a "sinful" woman to
publicly express her love and appreciation to Him by anointing
His feet in the home of Simon the Pharisee. In this simple but
unprecedented act, Jesus demonstrates His unconditional love,

grace, and forgiveness for *all* sinners. Knowing that Jesus saw her as a person of worth in her own right, and not merely as a sex object to be exploited and despised, inspired one of the most legendary acts of faith and devotion. Again and again in the Bible, we see women, whose lives have become destroyed because of sexual sin, being redeemed and restored to the glory of God.

So, why don't we see that happening today?

These ground-breaking and encouraging stories are as relevant today as they were two thousand years ago. Maybe more so. We need to stop shaming women by asking unhelpful questions such as, *Why* would any woman want to watch porn?, and start asking, *How* can we help? How can we create a guilt-free, shame-free environment that will encourage women and girls to come out of the shadows, to face their demons head-on, and be set free from their sin through the power of Christ and His gospel?

Can you ask your pastor to mention that women struggle with porn too when he next preaches on sexual issues? Can you bring the topic up for discussion in women's ministry? Can you bring a speaker into your women's and youth groups? Can you ask why there is a ministry for men, but not for women? Can you compile a list of resources and give them to your church?

When I brought a young female addict in to speak at my church, I later heard from a mom that her *ten-year-old* girl had broken down in tears on the way home and confessed her secret struggle with porn. That night the power of darkness was broken off that precious child. Many people had played a role in making that happen: the pastor's administrative assistant who asked me to give a presentation in the first place; the pastor and the elder board who gave the topic the go-ahead; Lily, the young female addict who willingly gave her testimony; the people who reposted the event on their social media pages; and the friend who had tagged all her daughter's friends' parents.

You don't have to get up on stage and give a presentation to make a difference. By simply bringing up the topic with friends and family you are shining the light. You have no way of knowing who in your circles is currently fighting a battle, alone, secretly in the dark. But rest assured, they are there. In your mommy groups. In your small group. In your work place. In your social media groups. In your youth group. For those who are unable to pull themselves out of the mud, it's up to all of us to stretch ourselves, form a chain, and grab their hands.

And if you are struggling, I want you to know that you are not alone. God sees you in your chains and in your struggle and wants to enter in it and tell you that you can be free. You may feel like that woman at the well, but that's a good thing because Jesus—*God in the flesh*—is known to show up at wells to set people free. Let Him meet you there.

CHAPTER 10

♥   ♥   ♥

Porn-Proofing Your Kids

Until the age of ten I grew up in home filled with second-hand smoke. My earliest childhood memories are of a yellow fog billowing out of my father's home office. But when my elder sister's asthma turned serious, my father quit his forty-a-day habit overnight.

Now thirty years later, thanks to an effective public health campaign, smoking is now banned from all public spaces and is far more discouraged in homes. Few people intentionally raise their child in an environment that they know is unhealthy.

However, when it comes to the issue of second-hand porn in our homes, there is still a collective blind spot despite the overwhelming evidence that parents' porn consumption negatively impacts children. I have never once heard it mentioned on the mommy-circuit. Have you? Discussions about keeping your marriage alive with date-nights? Frequently. The importance of keeping nitrates, BPAs, and artificial dyes out of the kitchen? Occasionally. But the dangers of porn in the home? Not once.

If you think about it, it's not that surprising. With more than 45 percent of Christians admitting that pornography is a major problem in the home,[1] the negative impact of second-hand porn on our kids is an extremely sensitive and taboo topic.

Believe me, if I could spare you this chapter, I would. Dealing with this issue in your marriage is hard enough without bringing kids into it. My mother's heart aches at the thought of you reading this and thinking about your own children. But I would be doing you a disservice if I didn't arm you with all the facts.

Deep breath, stay with me, I promise there is hope and good news to come.

The Direct Effects of Porn Consumption in the Family Home

With new research[2] coming out all the time, it is surprising how little air-time is given to highlighting the alarming effects of porn consumption in a household. The following effects are not subjective opinion, they are substantiated data.

- **Increased risk of accidental exposure to porn.** Children in homes where porn is consumed are more likely to be accidently exposed than children in homes where it is not. To a tender heart and an innocent mind, exposure to porn is traumatic and dangerous.

- **Porn activates the sexual part of a child's feeling-brain before their thinking-brain even knows what sex is.** That can set up a very confusing and compelling curiosity that may drive children to seek out more and more pornography.

- **Early exposure causes a higher risk of developing addictive sexual behavior and an earlier start to sexual activity.** Adolescent boys become more violent, aggressive, and sexually forward with peers, and adolescent girls are more inclined to tolerate emotional, physical, and sexual abuse.

- **Changes a child's view of sex overall.** Porn teaches children that sexual satisfaction is attainable without having affection for one's partner, and that extreme sex practices are common and desirable. Getting married and having a family is not seen as important or even desirable, much less a necessary and safe context for expressing sexuality.

The Indirect Impact of Parental Porn Use

Even if children are not exposed to porn as a direct result of a parent's habit, they are still indirectly impacted by the marital conflict it causes. Porn is the quiet killer of families, slowly and progressively destroying trust and intimacy between mothers and fathers. Going by current divorce rates, obsessive porn use contributes to half a million divorces a year.[3]

It is natural to want to shield your kids from the truth when it involves compulsive porn use, but experts say that it is actually worse for the child to be kept in the dark. Pretending that everything is fine will backfire.

Although parents may try to cover up marital conflict, children can sense the discord and often feel alone, anxious, depressed, and stressed. Children might isolate themselves, believing that they are somehow responsible. They become preoccupied with working out what is going on, and focusing on anything else becomes challenging. Even thinking, itself, becomes difficult. Their social, emotional, and cognitive development suffers as does their academic performance.[4] This discord affects their ability to cope, not just with the conflict but also with everyday stressors. In short, your kids know something is up. And they are trying to figure out what to do to fix it.

Please don't despair if any of this is ringing true in your family. There *is* a way to turn this around. Start talking about what is going on under the surface. The lies in your child's head must be broken with the truth, difficult and painful though it may be. I know this is tough to read, but maybe, just maybe, this is the nudge you need to finally tackle the issue of porn in your marriage.

Every time Satan whispers in your ear that it is pointless to try—that your husband (or you) is never going to change—think about the God who says nothing is impossible; and remind yourself that when you fight the porn in your home, you are siding with God. Who can stand against you when you side with God? Also, envision the healthy and porn-free family that your kids deserve and need, and focus on that.

Breaking the Generational Curse of Porn in Your Family

When it comes to protecting our children from becoming addicted to porn, most experts agree on a two-pronged attack. First, create an external filter by ensuring that access to explicit material is blocked on all devices. Second, create an internal filter in your child through education, which for a Christian includes the spiritual aspects of pornography. These are both effective and valuable steps. However, I would argue that there is also a third, even more vital, step.

Get porn out of your marriage.

From a spiritual perspective, this makes perfect sense. How can you begin to protect your household from a spirit of pornography when your husband (or you) keeps leaving the front door wide open? Studies reveal that children who grow up in the homes of addicts have increased likelihood of becoming addicted themselves.[5] Pornography addiction is a generational curse that will continue to affect your line until someone steps in and breaks it. This is your cue. When you take a stand against porn, you are not only siding with God and fighting to save your marriage, but also to change the entire future trajectory of your family.

Ready for that good news I promised?

You are uniquely equipped, and perfectly positioned, to help your children. By allowing your kids to witness your courage in fighting your own battle against porn, you will empower them to fight their own. By being honest and vulnerable with them you allow them to be honest and vulnerable with you. Here is an incredible opportunity to take the Enemy's favorite weapon, chop it up, and use it as fuel to transform your family for generations to come.

> When my twelve-year-old son came to me and confessed that he had been looking at porn, I was devastated. After everything I had just been through with my husband, I couldn't bear the thought of him heading down the same route. But as I held my gangly sobbing boy, I couldn't help feeling overwhelmingly grateful that he had come to me and confessed. As hard as it was to hear, his dark secret was out. It had lost its power over him. How different my husband's life might have been if he had been able to share his struggle at twelve.
>
> My son doesn't live in shame and fear anymore. Quite the opposite. Last month he gave his testimony to a bunch of kids at

*youth group. I have never been prouder of
him.* (Claire, age 38)

In my husband's profession as a Certified Sexual Addiction
Therapist, it is not unusual for him to be working with several
generations of the same family. It only takes one brave couple
to get the ball rolling. Once they start sharing their story with
those closest to them, others begin to believe that freedom and
transformation is possible in their own relationships. Siblings,
children, parents, all come forward and ask for help.

Gradually, and after a lot of work, the whole family system
is transformed. Isn't that just the most incredible thing you
have ever read? Don't you want an invite to that family home
at Thanksgiving? I know I do. I want to be at the table where
multi-generations have been set free, and for the first time they
are able to be truly present and appreciate and enjoy each other.

Going on the Offensive

It's time to talk strategy. Getting porn out of your marriage
is a vital component, but on its own, it is not enough to protect
your children from porn. You also need to go on the offensive.

The virtual sphere our children inhabit is barely recognizable
to the world we grew up in. On a daily basis, our kids face
challenges way beyond anything we had to deal with at their age.
The Enemy's weapons have been significantly upgraded and he
isn't shy about using them on children.

There's nothing quite like reading about the ways our kids
are being targeted by the porn industry to bring out my Mama

Bear. They understand that the best way to get customers for life is to hook them young. Take "typo-squatting," for instance, also known as URL hi-jacking. This is a common strategy used to trick young children onto a porn site when the link they are trying to type into their web browser has an accidental typo in it.

Likewise, "Metatagging" is another tactic, where words like *Santa Claus*, *Disneyland*, and *Teletubbies* are integrated into sites to draw children in when they are searching for those terms. Despite what I think about the morality of such practices, I cannot deny their effectiveness. Just look at where we are at:

- One in ten porn users are under the age of ten.[6]
- Ninety percent of nine- to sixteen-year-olds have been exposed to porn while doing their homework.[7]
- One in ten seventh graders are worried that they might be addicted to porn.[8]
- Average age of first exposure to porn is eleven. Other studies say the figure is closer to eight.[9]

It's hard not to choke on these statistics. When I think about my playful eight-year-old—who still loves to dress up and build blanket forts—being statistically only a few years away from being exposed to porn, it makes the top of my head nearly blow off.

Our kids need our guidance and protection in a way that we didn't require from our own parents. Before the Internet, porn was restricted both in terms of content and availability. Now the most violent and depraved porn imaginable is only a few clicks away, and it's not just available if they "happen" upon it or are looking for it. It's intentionally looking for them. As it stands, the only thing standing between your child and unlimited porn is your diligence.

Public awareness about the dangers of porn is gaining traction, but it's still very much in its infancy. As of Spring 2019, only fifteen states have passed resolutions that recognize the public health harms of pornography. The rest will follow, eventually. I have to believe that sooner or later our children will be educated about the dangers of porn as part of the course, along with smoking and other drugs. But I can't afford to wait for this to come to pass, and neither can you.

Despite feeling uncomfortable and unqualified to help our children navigate a pornified world, we don't have a choice. Porn is an equal opportunity toxin. Don't be lulled into a false sense of security just because your kid is an A-student, goes to church, has a relationship with God, and enjoys lots of friends and hobbies. Let me repeat that, porn can be enticing and addictive to any child. Remember Lily, the young female addict from the last chapter? Here's the story from her heartbroken mother's perspective.

> My husband and I did not know of our daughter's porn addiction until more than six years after she'd stumbled onto it on the computer. In the fifth grade at the time, she didn't know what to make of what she saw

and was too ashamed to tell us. A straight-A student at her Christian school, a swimmer and ballet dancer, actively involved in church, and especially warm and loving to us, she seemed the model child, so we couldn't understand her mood swings, depression, suicidal thoughts, and acting out. Little did we know that she despised herself and her ugly secret, and little did she know that rejection and debilitating pain in key relationships had made her susceptible to the lure of porn.

Where other pre-teen and adolescent girls engage in self-destructive acts to cope with pain, such as cutting, binge eating, and promiscuity, our daughter had found a private pornographic world. Never in our wildest imagination would we have thought it possible that a beloved ten-year-old child would become ensnared in the quicksand of porn. And never would we have believed that she could keep us in the dark for so many years. To support her addiction, she became a master of deception and disguise, playing one role for the outside world and slipping into another role in the privacy of her room, a duplicity that plunged her into despair. Consumed by shame, guilt, and disgust, she engaged in risky behavior, only exacerbating her low self-esteem until she no longer wanted to live.

Once we discovered her addiction, we were able to unravel the complex emotional issues that had made her vulnerable and begin the hard work of rehabilitating her warped view of relationships—and of herself and God. Hers is a story we wish would never have happened, a story we faulted ourselves for, but in God's hands, our pain was turned into praise. Today, she is a vibrant, healthy adult, able to forge meaningful relationships and only too glad to share her story of God's redemptive love so that others might know victory over addiction.

I personally know this family. They are the sort of parents I could only dream of being. This tragedy really can happen to anyone. I don't say this to frighten you, but to motivate you to take action. This family did not talk about porn with their daughter simply because it never crossed their mind that it would ever be a problem.

Even if your son or daughter appears perfectly capable of making good decisions, when it comes to having access to porn, there are four good reasons why *you* have to do the thinking for them.

Why Teenagers Are Particularly Susceptible to Porn

Their brain is still developing

When children are small, there are constant reminders that their brains are still developing. Every few minutes brings another example of how they are unable to reason; how they do not understand cause and effect; and how their immediate desire supersedes any notion of what they know to be right from wrong. It is obvious that parents (or guardians) have to think for them in this phase of life and teach them how to think as they develop. Who else is going to make sure they wear warm clothes, put on sunscreen, and stop them walking out into the road?

While this lack of mental ability is readily accepted in young children, it is not as widely understood that, to a lesser degree, these developmental shortcomings still exist in our teenagers. When they are towering over us with an answer for everything, it is easy to forget that their brains are still developing. There is a good reason they do not have it all figured out yet. Remember, the prefrontal cortex (the command center) is not fully developed under the age of twenty-five.

The next time you, in sheer exasperation, think *What on earth is wrong with you?*, remember teenagers have underdeveloped abilities to delay gratification, understand consequences, and weigh options. Ever wonder why car insurance drops down after the age of twenty-five? Now you know.

Highest level of testosterone

Teenagers naturally produce a chemical combo that makes them extra impulsive and extra sexual. A teenage boy at age eighteen or nineteen has more testosterone in his system than at any other time in his life.[10] Testosterone is the "make things happen" hormone, the chemical that drives men to compete, argue, persevere, to have sex. I'm not making boys the enemy here or calling them animals by any stretch of the imagination—I am simply stating how their body is changing and developing at this age. The surge of testosterone is real, and it's up to us as parents to help them navigate it.

Abnormally high levels of dopamine

Teenagers also have an abnormally high level of the neurotransmitter dopamine. This is the brain chemical that motivates us and makes us much more impulsive. Teenagers are biologically and neurochemically more impulsive, more sexual, and less able to reason. This doesn't mean that they are incapable of making judgment calls, it doesn't mean they are incapable of being godly, and it doesn't mean they aren't responsible for their actions. But it does mean that they are in a fragile and volatile place in this season of life and need to lean on their parents (and other trustworthy adults) for strength, consistency, and perspective.

Post pubescence is a critical time of restructuring in the brain

The teenage years are a time of heavy lifting in the brain—a time of major restructuring. This is when the brain decides which neural pathways to strengthen and which to let atrophy. Any activity that is "fun," or activates dopamine, is naturally given precedence. Because of the insane levels of dopamine that accompany porn, the neural pathways associated with it are *super* strengthened. Soon math, Spanish, baseball, guitar, even hanging out with friends, will all take a back seat to porn. It is important to understand that the effect of heavy consumption of porn during these critical years can be profound and long-lasting.

> The capacity of a teen to wire up new sexual associations mushrooms around age 11–12 for girls, 12–13 for boys, when billions of new neural connections (synapses) create endless possibilities. However, by adulthood his brain will have pruned his neural circuitry to leave him with a manageable assortment of choices. By his twenties, he may not exactly be *stuck* with the sexual proclivities he falls into during adolescence, but they can be like deep ruts in his brain—not easy to ignore or reconfigure.[11]

What Are the Tell-Tale Signs That
My Child Is Watching Porn?

A parent's best line of defense is vigilance. When monitoring your child's online behavior, knowing what to look out for is half the battle. Put the following signs on your radar. They may reveal that your child is on the way to becoming addicted, if they are not addicted already.

Increase in Pop-ups

Most porn websites make money from pop-up advertisements. If you notice that the number of pop-ups has increased, it's probably because someone in the family is regularly accessing porn.

Rapidly Closing Programs or Staring at Desktop

There is nothing more suspicious that walking into your child's room only to find them staring at their desktop wallpaper. Be warned, kids can get really good at rapidly closing down windows and hiding what they are doing. I have heard stories of homeschooled children watching porn with their mother in the same room.

Staying up Late

Consistently staying up late surfing the web is a big red-flag, as is accessing a device in an isolated location within the home, such as their bedroom or a basement.

Long Showers

If your child is taking extra-long showers, it might be worth checking if they are taking their phone or another mobile device in the bathroom with them.

Changes in Behavior

This is where your mommy instinct comes in. Do you feel that your child has become uncharacteristically secretive and defensive? Do they keep to themselves in their room?

With younger kids, the transformation is often more marked and sudden. Children change overnight from being outgoing and happy, to being withdrawn and acting out aggressively with siblings and at school.

Deleted Browsing History

A child who has nothing to hide does not need to delete their browser history. Asking your child to explain why there is no history will tell you everything. This is easier checked on computers in the home, but for personal devices, you may need to seek help from monitoring apps.

Choosing the Right Parental Controls

It's easy to feel intimidated by rapidly changing technology, and when it comes to comparing and contrasting all the technological solutions for filtering, blocking, and accountability, it is just as overwhelming. If only there was a website that would just tell you what was the best for your family situation. Well, here's some great news—there is!

Check out: www.protectyoungeyes.com/parental-control. This life-saving, free resource provides a comprehensive plan of attack tailored to the devices your child uses. Recommendations are kept up-to-date, and the step-by-step instructions are straightforward. Every time I found myself confused by an unfamiliar term, there was a handy link to another article that helped explain it to me.

What I particularly like about this website is that it recommends the best software to fit your situation, based on the ages of your children and what you are seeking to accomplish. Do you need a strong filter for young Internet users (or those who are tech savvy)? Do you have trouble with inappropriate YouTube use? Do you just want to manage screen time or block certain apps? Do you need accountability software to facilitate conversations with an older child who is transitioning into more independence online?

My top piece of tech advice to parents is to ensure that you restrict your child's ability to download apps onto their phone without your knowledge. You need to keep on top of what black holes your child has access to. A quick Google search on "Dangerous apps for kids," will get you up to speed on the latest dirty dozen. Be aware that there are hidden porn vaults that are designed to look like innocent apps, like a calculator or audio manager. I know, shocking, right? You also need to know it is possible to get around Internet filters and onto the web through perfectly legit apps like the weather app.

A final word of caution: if your child is determined to find porn, and they are more tech savvy than you, chances are they will be able to find a way around any Internet filter you install. A quick Google search of the "Easy ways kids get around Internet filters" will confirm this. External filters are important but creating an internal filter in the heart is crucial.

Creating an Internal Filter

Along with road safety, stranger-danger, and the underwear rule, porn-proofing our kids is just another responsibility that parents now have. Experts agree that the optimum time to start teaching your kids about porn is before you have to. With the average age of exposure being somewhere between eight and eleven, depending on who you listen to, this means starting young. For every fourteen-year-old that stumbled upon porn while doing their homework, there is also a five-year-old who misspelled "Dora the Explorer" on Google and was deliberately re-directed to a porn site.

My husband and I decided to have our first little chat about porn when our oldest was seven and our youngest was five. For sure, it certainly felt weird and more than a little sad to have to talk about "bad pictures" in between a trip to the firehouse open day and an episode of *Spiderman*, but I knew there was never going to be a time when I felt okay with talking about porn with my kids. This Mama Bear desperately wants to shield them from all the awful things of the world for as long as possible.

If you feel that you wouldn't know where to start with a conversation like this, fear not. Help is at hand in the form of a picture book called *Good Pictures, Bad Pictures Jr.: A Simple Plan to Protect Young Minds* by Kristen A. Jenson. This quick, easy-to-read picture book is aimed at children between the ages of three and six. Using gentle, age-appropriate messages, children learn to "Turn, Run, and Tell" when they are accidentally exposed to inappropriate content.

There is also an older version of the book aimed at kids over seven called *Good Pictures Bad Pictures: Porn-Proofing Today's Young Kids*. It explains what pornography is, *why* it's dangerous, and how to reject it. Using easy-to-understand science and simple analogies, it teaches kids how to porn-proof their own brains.

Taking this first baby step with my boys wasn't difficult at all. We cuddled up on the sofa, read the book, had a bit of discussion, and then went back to playing Star Wars. No big deal. Our next step is to rinse and repeat, gradually introducing more information as appropriate.

Porn-proofing your kids does not happen in a single conversation. It is an on-going dialogue. Sometimes you will get to plan your conversation and have all your resources lined up; at other times you will simply react to impromptu teachable moments. But even when your kids' dumb decisions trigger you, don't forget to take a few deep breaths before responding. Your goal here is to keep the channels open. You want your kids to come to you when they have questions about something they have seen.

So, how do you talk to older kids about porn? How do you convince your teen that this isn't about you being prudish or out of touch? How do you explain to them that porn will hurt them as an individual, and mess up their relationships in a way that they will hear?

Drum roll, please . . .

First, I am so excited to introduce you to www.fightthenew drug.org.

Fight the New Drug is a game-changing, non-religious, non-legislative, non-profit organization that exists to educate youth about the harmful effects of porn. Through school presentations, and a rapidly growing social media presence, they come alongside kids in an entertaining and relevant way to confront them with the ways porn is affecting their brains, their relationships, and the world around them. The website is stacked with terrific resources that explain tricky concepts far better than you or I could. Seriously, check it out. You will not be disappointed. I recommend you check out their interactive resource to help parents know how to address the topic of pornography with their kids. It's called "Let's Talk about Porn: A Conversation Blueprint," and you can find it at https://fightthenewdrug.org/lets-talk-about-porn/.

Here are two other wonderful options to help guide your ongoing conversation:

- Fight the New Drug's three-part documentary series called *Brain, Heart, World*. It is free for individuals to stream, and available to purchase for public screenings.

Filled with compelling teen testimonies and easy-to-understand explanations from leading world experts, these short films present a much-needed alternative narrative to the one being pumped at them through their devices. Plus, showing the films at your local school or church is such an easy way to educate your kid's friends, not to mention their parents. After all, it takes a village, right?

- Another fantastic resource for educating yourself alongside your child is www.yourbrainonporn.com. They have fascinating videos that go further into the science behind porn addiction. This website is a great recalibration tool for living in this crazy world. Whenever I read seductive pro-porn propaganda and feel my convictions getting disorientated, five minutes scrolling through the hundreds of research studies on this well-maintained site gets my head straight.

Lastly, don't forget how important it is to present a biblical counter-narrative to porn. In today's porn-saturated world you cannot leave your children to make sense of sex on their own. To help your child understand porn as an evil distortion of God's beautiful creation, you need to present the biblical vision for sex. One where sex is not a dirty word, but a life-affirming, passionate expression of love within marriage, designed by a loving God in His wisdom and goodness. Conversations about the negatives of pursuing pornography must be balanced by celebrating and promoting God's good intentions for a fulfilling and satisfying sex-life with your spouse.

Support for a Child Who Is Struggling

Remember: a child who is struggling with compulsive porn use is a child whose brain has been hijacked. Satan will happily use this situation to guilt you into paralysis, or turn your fear to anger, but do not fall for his lies. Your parenting has all sorts of sin issues in it, I'm sure, but when it comes to this, your parenting did not create this—you did not lead them to this well and make them drink. And your child, I'm sure, has all sorts of sin issues inside as well. But again, they did not create this. They may have given into it or chosen it after being exposed, but they did not get up in the morning and decide they wanted to be addicted to degrading and harmful images that would rip their heart and brain and family apart. Yes, we all have our sin to deal with, and we *should*. But the truth is, your kids were targeted. The problem is porn.

If your child was literally being held hostage, I know you would fight relentlessly to free them. Without thinking twice, you would do whatever it took to get them back. When it comes to rescuing your child from porn, you need the same focus and determination. Channel your inner Liam Neeson. If you need to take away their phone and other privileges, do it. If you have to enforce consequences for lying, do it. When your child complains, grit your teeth and close your ears. It's only the porn talking anyway, and you do not negotiate with terrorists.

For a kid who is occasionally dabbling in porn, but is not yet addicted, installing accountability software might be enough of a deterrent. But if you have a kid that just can't stop, you can do the following:

- Lock down their access to the Internet
- Get them a mentor
- Find a support group (in person or online https://www.joinfortify.com/legacy)
- Educate them about porn
- Do a full disclosure
- Create a safety plan

However, in cases when a child is in so deep that they don't even want to be free, you will need to seek professional help. Contact a local certified sexual addiction therapist for recommendations. If your child is fighting you all the way, *you* are going to need support too.

No matter what your situation is, your children need you to get porn out of your marriage and home, and go on the offensive. When parents are unable to present a united front, implementing and enforcing necessary boundaries becomes even harder. This is not to say that a single parent can't be effective on their own. Indeed, it is much more effective to have one strong parent than two giving mixed messages.

Either way, it's time to become a warrior. Unleash your Mama Bear and go save your child. You can do it.

I know I've hit you with a lot of information in this chapter, and I get how overwhelming the fight seems. Porn is moving into weirder and more disturbing territory faster than we can keep up: virtual reality, sex robots, deep-fake porn, spy cams, personalized snap-chat porn, you name it. Just when I think I've heard it all, I open up my newsfeed and . . . *bam*, I am shaking my head in disbelief again.

My husband and I are on the cusp on entering the fray for real with our own two boys. And probably because I have read more books about this subject than is good for me, I can easily slip into fear and panic. In my own strength I feel like David, small and weak, facing a gigantic enemy with nothing more than a slingshot. But then I remember that with God on his side all David needed to defeat Goliath was to be willing to fight, and to remember his slingshot.

Whatever fronts you are currently fighting porn on—in your marriage, in your kids, in your mind, or possibly all three—all you need is a willingness to fight, and a slingshot. With God on your side, fear not. Pack that sling with all the lies and fears that have been holding you back, and let it fly. Walk boldly in the light about all your struggles, and confess your sins in full confidence that the battle is already won. God will deliver you, dazzle you, and put praise upon your lips. He can do this. He's done it for me and countless others. Friend, sister, mom, daughter, roommate: go fight for love.

> The Lord GOD will wipe away the tears from
> every face and remove his people's disgrace from
> the whole earth, for the LORD has spoken. On

that day it will be said, "Look, this is our God; we have waited for him, and he has saved us. This is the Lord; we have waited for him. Let us rejoice and be glad in his salvation." For the Lord's power will rest on this mountain. (Isa. 25:8–10)

Notes

Introduction

1. J. Dedmon, "Is the Internet bad for your marriage? Online affairs, pornographic sites playing greater role in divorces," Press Release from The Dilenschneider Group, Inc. (Nov. 2002).

Chapter 1

1. Andre Mitchell, "Porn-Has-Become-Greatest-Threat-to-Christs-Cause-in-Modern-World-Christian-Author-Warns," *ChristianityToday.com*, 9 Apr. 2016, www.christianitytoday.com/.

2. Proven Men, "Pornography Survey Statistics," www.proven men.org/pornography-survey-statistics-2014/.

3. Ibid.

4. Chyng Sun, Ana Bridges, Jennifer Johnason, and Matt Ezzell, "Pornography and the Male Sexual Script: An Analysis of Consumption and Sexual Relations," *Archives of Sexual Behavior* 45, no. 4 (2014): 983–94.

5. D. Zillmann and J. Bryant, "Pornography's impact on sexual satisfaction," *Journal of Applied Social Psychology* 18 (1988):438–53.

6. Valerie Voon et al., "Neural Correlates of Sexual Cue Reactivity in Individuals with and without Compulsive Sexual

Behaviours," *PLoS ONE*, vol. 9, no. 7 (2014) doi:10.1371/journal .pone.0102419.

7. Brian Park, Brian et al., "Is Internet Pornography Causing Sexual Dysfunctions? A Review with Clinical Reports," *Behavioral Sciences,* vol. 6, no. 3 (2016): 17, doi:10.3390/bs6030017.

8. Amanda M. Maddox et al., "Viewing Sexually-Explicit Materials Alone or Together: Associations with Relationship Quality," *SpringerLink*, Springer, Dordrecht, 29 Dec. 2009, link. springer.com/article/10.1007/s10508-009-9585-4.

9. D. Zillmann, "The effects of prolonged consumption of pornography," in: D. Zillmann, J. Bryant, eds., *Pornography: Research Advances and Policy Considerations* (Hillsdale, NJ: Lawrence Erlbaum, 1989), 127–57.

10. Samuel L. Perry and Cyrus Schleifer, "Till Porn Do Us Part? A Longitudinal Examination of Pornography Use and Divorce," *The Journal of Sex Research*, vol. 55, no. 3 (2017): 284–96, doi:10.1080/00224499.2017.1317709.

11. S. Stack, I. Wasserman, and R. Kern, "Adult Social Bonds and Use of Internet Pornography," *Social Science Quarterly* 85 (2004): 75–88.

Chapter 2

1. Deirdre Barrett, *Supernormal Stimuli: How Primal Urges Overran Their Evolutionary Purpose* (New York: W. W. Norton, 2010).

2. N. D. Volkow et al., "Neurobiologic Advances from the Brain Disease Model of Addiction," *The New England Journal of Medicine,* U.S. National Library of Medicine, 28 Jan. 2016, www .ncbi.nlm.nih.gov/pubmed/26816013.

3. Valerie Voon et al., "Neural Correlates of Sexual Cue Reactivity in Individuals with and without Compulsive Sexual

Behaviours," *PLOS Medicine*, Public Library of Science, journals. plos.org/plosone/article?id=10.1371%2Fjournal.pone.0102419.

4. Volkow et al., "Neurobiologic Advances from the Brain Disease Model of Addiction."

5. Ibid.

6. D. A. Dewsbury, "Effects of Novelty of Copulatory Behavior: The Coolidge Effect and Related Phenomena," *Psychological Bulletin* 89, no. 3 (1981): 464–82.

7. "Desensitization: A Numbed Pleasure Response," *Start Here: Evolution Has Not Prepared Your Brain for Today's Porn | Your Brain on Porn,* www.yourbrainonporn.com/book/export/html/702.

8. Brian Park et al., "Is Internet Pornography Causing Sexual Dysfunctions? A Review with Clinical Reports," *MDPI,* Multidisciplinary Digital Publishing Institute, 5 Aug. 2016, www .mdpi.com/2076-328X/6/3/17/htm.

9. E. J. Nestler, "Is There a Common Molecular Pathway for Addiction?" *Nature Neuroscience*, U.S. National Library of Medicine (Nov. 2005), www.ncbi.nlm.nih.gov/pubmed/16251986.

10. Todd Love et al., "Neuroscience of Internet Pornography Addiction: A Review and Update," MDPI, Multidisciplinary Digital Publishing Institute, 18 Sept. 2015, www.mdpi.com/2076 -328X/5/3/388.

11. Volkow et al, "Neurobiologic Advances from the Brain Disease Model of Addiction."

12. Ibid.

13. G. Wilson, "Behavioral Addictions," *Start Here: Evolution Has Not Prepared Your Brain for Today's Porn | Your Brain on Porn*, www.yourbrainonporn.com/behavioral-addictions.

14. Norman Doidge, *The Brain That Changes Itself* (New York: Penguin Books, 2007), 242–43.

15. Eric J. Nestler, "Transcriptional Mechanisms of Addiction: Role of ΔFosB," *Philosophical Transactions of the Royal Society B:*

Biological Sciences, The Royal Society, 12 Oct. 2008, rstb.royal
societypublishing.org/content/363/1507/3245.

16. Kyle K. Pitchers et al., "Natural and Drug Rewards Act
on Common Neural Plasticity Mechanisms with ΔFosB as a Key
Mediator," *Journal of Neuroscience,* Society for Neuroscience, 20
Feb. 2013, www.jneurosci.org/content/33/8/3434.

17. Laier Love et al., "Neuroscience of Internet Pornography
Addiction: A Review and Update," *Behavioral Sciences* 5, no. 3
(2015): 388–433.

18. N. D. Volkow and M. Morales, "The Brain on Drugs: From
Reward to Addiction," *Cell* 162, no. 8 (2015): 713.

19. Kent C. Berridge and Terry E. Robinson, "Liking, Wanting,
and the Incentive-Sensitization Theory of Addiction," *Current
Biology,* Cell Press, 1 Nov. 2016, experts.umich.edu/en/publications
/liking-wanting-and-the-incentive-sensitization-theory-of-addictio.

20. Doidge, *The Brain That Changes Itself,* 242–43.

21. Aline Wery and J. Billieux, "Online Sexual Activities: An
Exploratory Study of Problematic and Non-Problematic Usage
Patterns in a Sample of Men," *Computers in Human Behavior,*
Pergamon, 14 Dec. 2015, www.sciencedirect.com/science/article/pii
/S0747563215302612.

22. Gary Wilson, "Hypofrontality," *Start Here: Evolution Has
Not Prepared Your Brain for Today's Porn | Your Brain on Porn,* www
.yourbrainonporn.com/garys-research-hypofrontality.

23. Seog Ju Kim et al., "Prefrontal Grey-Matter Changes in
Short-Term and Long-Term Abstinent Methamphetamine Abusers,"
The International Journal of Neuropsychopharmacology 9, no. 02
(2005): 221.

24. Doidge, *The Brain That Changes Itself.*

Chapter 4

1. Josh McDowell, *The Porn Phenomenon: The Impact of Pornography in the Digital Age* (Ventura, CA: Barna Group, 2016), 117.

Chapter 5

1. Jennifer P. Schneider, www.jenniferschneider.com/articles/surviving_disclosure.html.

2. Stephanie Carnes, ed., *Mending a Shattered Heart: A Guide for Partners of Sex Addicts* (Carefree, AZ: Gentle Path Press, 2011), 96–101.

3. Patrick Carnes, *Sexual Anorexia* (Center City, MN: Hazelden, 1997), 1.

Chapter 6

1. Timothy Keller, *The Meaning of Marriage: Facing the Complexities of Commitment with the Wisdom of God* (New York: Penguin Group, 2011), 95.

Chapter 7

1. Pia Mellody et al., *Facing Codependence: What It Is, Where It Comes from, How It Sabotages Our Lives* (HarperSanFrancisco, 2003), 4–6.

Chapter 8

1. https://blog.godreports.com/2016/01/josh-mcdowell-says-porn-epidemic-sweeping-the-church/

2. Josh McDowell, *The Porn Phenomenon: The Impact of Pornography in the Digital Age* (Ventura, CA: Barna Group, 2016), 100.

3. Ibid., 115.

4. Ana J. Bridges et al., "Aggression and Sexual Behavior in Best-Selling Pornography Videos: A Content Analysis Update," *Violence Against Women* 16, no. 10 (2019): 1065–1085, doi:10 .1177/1077801210382866.

5. K. Ohbuchi, T. Ikeda, and G. Takeuchi, "Effects of violent pornography upon viewers rape myth beliefs: A study of Japanese males," *Psychology, Crime & Law* 1 (1994): 71–81.

6. Theodore G. Tappert, trans. and ed., *Luther: Letters of Spiritual Counsel* (Vancouver, BC: Regent College Publishing, 2003).

Chapter 9

1. "World's Largest Porn Site Reveals What Type of Porn Women Watch," *Fight the New Drug*, 12 Mar. 2018, fightthenewdrug.org/ worlds-largest-porn-site-reveals-what-women-are-watching/.

2. Proven Men, "Pornography Survey Statistics," www.proven men.org/pornography-survey-statistics-2014/.

3. Josh McDowell, *The Porn Phenomenon* (Ventura, CA: Barna Group, 2016).

4. I. P. Albery et al., "Exploring the Relationship between Sexual Compulsivity and Attentional Bias to Sex-Related Words in a Cohort of Sexually Active Individuals," *Eur Addict Res* 23(2017):1–6." Karger Publisher, 2016, www.karger.com/Article/ Abstract/448732.

5. Kate Julian, "Why Are Young People Having So Little Sex?" *The Atlantic,* Atlantic Media Company, 17 May 2019, www.the atlantic.com/magazine/archive/2018/12/the-sex-recession/573949/.

6. "What Women Want," *Pornhub Insights*, 4 Jan. 2019, www. pornhub.com/insights/what-women-want.

7. Kayt Sukel, "The Neuroscience of Porn Viewing," *The Huffington Post*, TheHuffingtonPost.com, 26 Mar. 2013, www.

huffingtonpost.com/kayt-sukel/the-neuroscience-of-porn-viewing
_b_2955650.html.

8. Roxanne Khamsi, "Women Become Sexually Aroused as Quickly as Men," *New Scientist*, www.newscientist.com/article/ dn10213-women-become-sexually-aroused-as-quickly-as-men/.

9. Michael Leahy, *Porn University: What College Students Are Really Saying about Sex on Campus* (Chicago: Northfield Publishing, 2009).

10. Michael Le Page, "Orgasms: A Real 'Turn-off' for Women," *New Scientist*, 20 June 2005, www.newscientist.com/article/dn7548 -orgasms-a-real-turn-off-for-women/.

11. Heather A. Rupp and Kim Wallen, "Sex Differences in Response to Visual Sexual Stimuli: A Review," Archives of Sexual Behavior, U.S. National Library of Medicine, Apr. 2008, www.ncbi .nlm.nih.gov/pmc/articles/PMC2739403.

12. Rosalind Gill, "From Sexual Objectification to Sexual Subjectification: The Resexualisation of Women's Bodies in the Media," http://mrzine.monthlyreview.org/2009/gill230509.html.

13. Initially this content was found on a few Jessica Harris blog posts. I then amalgamated her words and asked her permission for this, requesting if I could quote her. She agreed to these quotations via email correspondence with me.

Chapter 10

1. Paul Coughlin, "Pornography and Virtual Infidelity," *Focus on the Family*, 8 Jan. 2009, www.focusonthefamily.com/marriage /divorce-and-infidelity/pornography-and-virtual-infidelity/virtual -infidelity-and-marriage.

2. Jill C. Manning, "The Impact of Internet Pornography on Marriage and the Family: A Review of the Research, Sexual Addiction & Compulsivity," (2006) 13:2–3, 131–65, DOI: 10.1080 /10720160600870711.

3. Kevin B. Skinner, "Is Porn Really Destroying 500,000 Marriages Annually?" *Psychology Today*, Sussex Publishers, 12 Dec. 2011, Web, 23 July 2019.

4. G. T. Harold, J. J. Aitken, & K. H. Shelton, "Inter-parental conflict and children's academic attainment: a longitudinal analysis," (2007), https://www.ncbi.nlm.nih.gov/pubmed/18093028.

5. Jessica M. Solis, Julia M. Shadur, Alison R. Burns, and Andrea M. Hussong. "Understanding the Diverse Needs of Children Whose Parents Abuse Substances," *Current Drug Abuse Reviews*, U.S. National Library of Medicine, June 2012, Web, 23 July 2019.

6. "One in 10 Visitors to Hardcore Porn Sites Is Under 10 Years Old, Study Shows," *Fight the New Drug*, 30 July 2018, fightthenewdrug.org /data-says-one-in-10-visitors-to-porn-sites-are-under-10-years-old/.

7. "Pornography Statistics," *Family Safe*, www.familysafemedia. com/pornography-statistics/.

8. Kristin MacLaughlin, "The Detrimental Effects of Pornography on Small Children," *Net Nanny*, 19 Dec. 2017, www.netnanny.com/ blog/the-detrimental-effects-of-pornography-on-small-children/.

9. "What's the Average Age of a Kid's First Porn Exposure?" *Fight the New Drug*, 1 Mar. 2019, fightthenewdrug.org/real-average -age-of-first-exposure/.

10. Alexia Severson et al., "Testosterone Levels by Age: Normal Levels, Low T Signs, Women & More," *Healthline*, Healthline Media, 7 Nov. 2018, www.healthline.com/health/low-testosterone/ testosterone-levels-by-age#normal-testosterone-levels.

11. https://www.yourbrainonporn.com/relevant-research-and -articles-about-the-studies/adolescent-brain/.